*International Journal
for the
Study of the
Christian Church*

Volume 1   Number 1   2001

International Journal for the Study of
the Christian Church

An international, ecumenical, inter-disciplinary refereed journal, including commissioned and unsolicited articles, IJSCC will actively promote ecumenical discussion of and within the church, drawing on contributors from across the different Christian traditions. It will seek to provide a platform for discussion of the forms of the Church and its varied historical manifestations. Confessional approaches to the Church will have an important place in the journal.

The editors welcome articles and books for review in areas
such as the following:

the nature and identity of the Church

order and ministry

current thinking on ecclesiology and its bearing on the mission of the Church

the ecclesiological dimensions of sacramental and liturgical theology

ecumenical ecclesiology

the relationship between ecclesiology and other areas of Christian theology

methodological questions in ecclesiology

historical and biblical questions in ecclesiology

empirical studies of the Church

International Journal for the Study of the Christian Church

Volume 1   Number 1   2001

Editors
GEOFFREY ROWELL
PAUL AVIS
CHRISTINE HALL
ROBERT HANNAFORD

T&T CLARK
EDINBURGH & NEW YORK

T&T CLARK LTD

A Continuum imprint

59 George Street
Edinburgh EH2 2LQ
Scotland

www.tandtclark.co.uk

370 Lexington Avenue
New York 10017–6503
USA

www.continuumbooks.com

First published 2001

ISBN 0 567 08826 X
ISSN 1474 225X

British Library Cataloguing-in-Publication Data
A catalogue record for this book is available from the British Library

Typeset by Waverley Typesetters, Galashiels
Printed and bound in Great Britain by Bell & Bain Ltd, Glasgow

Contents

Contributors

PHILIP BOYCE, OCD, is a native of Ireland and a member of the Discalced Carmelites. He received a doctorate in theology (DD) in 1974 with a dissertation on the spirituality of John Henry Newman and was professor of spirituality and dogmatic theology in the Pontifical Theological Faculty of the Carmelites in Rome (the Teresianum). In 1995 he was ordained Bishop of Raphoe (County Donegal). Since 1975 he has collaborated with the 'Centre of Newman's Friends' in Rome and has written various articles on Newman and on Carmelite Spirituality. He has edited with introduction and notes the anthology *John Henry Newman, 'Mary'. The Virgin Mary in the Life and Writings of John Henry Newman* (Gracewing and Eerdmans, 2001).

DAVID BROWN is Van Mildert Professor of Divinity in the University of Durham, England and a Canon of Durham Cathedral. Among his many books are *The Divine Truth* (Duckworth, 1985) and two major studies on the nature of tradition and the significance of the imagination in Christian theology *Tradition and Imagination* (OUP, 1999) and *Discipleship and Imagination* (OUP, 2000).

FRANCIS McGRATH is an Australian Marist Brother and was the first Australian to complete doctoral work in Newman studies at Oxford. In the early 1980s he undertook post-graduate studies at Boston College, Mass., studying under Bernard Lonergan. His recent work in Australia has been to write and co-ordinate a national-wide distance theological education programme *Foundations: A Systematic Introduction to Theology*. He is the author of *John Henry Newman: Universal Revelation* (Burns & Oates, 1997).

JAMES PEREIRO is a priest of the Opus Dei Prelature and Chaplain of Grandpont House, Oxford. He holds an MA in history and a Doctorate in Education. His Doctoral Thesis in Theology was on Cano's *De Locis Theologicis*. Among his recent publications is *Cardinal Manning: an Intellectual Biography* (Clarendon Press, 1998).

GEOFFREY ROWELL is Anglican Bishop of Gibraltar in Europe and an Emeritus Fellow of Keble College, Oxford, where he taught 19th Century History and Theology in the University from 1972–1993. He is the author of *Hell and the Victorians* (Clarendon Press, 1974), *The Liturgy of Christian Burial* (Alcuin/SPCK, 1977; 2nd edition forthcoming) and *The Vision Glorious* (OUP, 1983) and co-editor of *Love's Redeeming Work: The Anglican Quest for Holiness* (OUP, 2001), a major anthology of Anglican spiritual readings.

PAUL VAISS was born of Jewish parents and attended a rabbinic school after he acknowledged Christ. He studied at the Sorbonne and wrote his doctoral thesis on the evolution of Newman's thought. He is Professor of English Civilisation and History of Ideas at Paris X University (Nanterre), and an evangelical Bible teacher and church leader. He is the author of *Newman: sa vie, sa pensée, et sa spiritualité: première période* (L'Hartmann, 1991) and is currently preparing a two-volume biography of Newman's Anglican years, in English.

HALBERT WEIDNER is a member of the Oratory of St Philip Neri, Dean of East Honolulu and Ecumenical Officer for the Roman Catholic Diocese of Honolulu, Hawaii. He is the author of two works on Newman and of a wide range of articles published in Roman Catholic and Ecumenical journals.

Editorial:
Newman and Ecclesiology

GEOFFREY ROWELL

I N the glossary to their *History of the Ecumenical Movement* Ruth Rouse and Stephen Neill write of the word 'Ecclesiology' that 'English dictionaries define this word as "the science of churches, esp. of church building and decoration". In recent years, under the influence of the German *Ekklesiologie*, it has come to be used not infrequently in the sense of "that part of dogmatic theology which deals with the nature and existence of the Church". It seems likely that this use will come to establish itself in good English.'[1] So indeed it has proved. The old English meaning of ecclesiology, current especially in the mid-nineteenth century, when *The Ecclesiologist* analysed and advised on church restorations and appropriate designs for piscinas and patens and urged that Early English was the normative Gothic architecture,[2] has long since been supplanted by 'ecclesiology' in the sense of 'the doctrine of the Church'.

There have been many contributing factors to this change, the seeds of which lie much further back in history. In the Reformation in the West national churches repudiating the claims of the papacy and the polity of mediaeval Catholicism sought a scriptural model of church organisation, and in doing so had to give their own account of church history. Reformation of churches always means a re-telling of church history. Inevitably churches defined themselves over against each other, appealing for justification to both scripture and tradition. The radical Reformation, repudiating

---

[1] R. Rouse and S. C. Neill (eds), *A History of the Ecumenical Movement, 1517–1948* (2nd edn, London: SPCK, 1967), p. 806.

[2] Cf. James F. White, *The Cambridge Movement: the Ecclesiologists and the Gothic Revival* (Cambridge: Cambridge University Press, 1962).

not just Rome, but the Erastianism of state control that so frequently replaced it, led to both congregational and 'spiritual' understandings of the Church. The quest for a pure church produced tensions similar to that of Donatism in the early centuries of the Church, and questions of power and control often became mingled with doctrines of ministry, as in James I's celebrated dictum, 'No bishop, no king!' The French Revolution and the consequent dissolution of the *ancien régime*, with the attack on the Church and Christianity that went with it, meant that all churches had to question their own identity, roots and character. The demise of the old confessional state, and the emergence of more pluralist European societies, meant that in different ways churches were forced to ask questions about their polities and the grounding of those polities in their foundation documents. Newman's question at the beginning of the Oxford Movement, 'On what ground do you stand, O presbyter of the Church of England?' could be reproduced in many different contexts. It was no accident that the nineteenth-century Roman Catholic Church saw the growth of Ultramontanism, with its appeal to Papal authority, an appeal that was materially helped by the growth of new and speedier communications. In England that same new ease of communications meant that even a denomination such as the Congregationalists, found it expedient to set up a Congregational Union in 1832, the year before John Keble preached the Assize Sermon on 'National Apostasy' that Newman reckoned as the beginning of the Oxford Movement. In 1881 another Congregationalist, J. Guinness Rogers, devoted major Congregational Union lectures to the theme of church systems in England. In a wide survey he gave extensive treatment to the Church of England and the English Free Churches but noted that he had not treated Ultramontanism (or indeed the Roman Catholic Church) because it was 'so distinctly a foreign system that I do not feel that its omission interferes with the completeness of the present survey'.[3] The Orthodox Churches, although understandably omitted from a survey of English churches at that time, do not gain even a passing mention.

The nineteenth century was also the age of imperial expansion, and with it of missionary endeavour. New churches in non-Christian environments demanded organisation raising in turn the issue of how churches were to be governed. The emergence of synodical government in Anglicanism owed much to the practical questions faced by George Augustus Selwyn (1809–78), the first bishop of New Zealand, and George Washington Doane (1799–1859), bishop of New Jersey, gave one of the earliest defini-

---

[3] J. Guinness Rogers, *Church Systems of England in the Nineteenth Century* (The Sixth Congregational Union Lecture) (London: Hodder & Stoughton, 1881), p. ix.

tions of a missionary bishop: 'a bishop *sent forth* by the Church, not *sought for of* the Church; going *before* to organise the Church, not waiting till the Church has been partially organised; a leader not a follower'.[4]

If Christian division, Christian missionary endeavour, and the changing relations between Church and society, in their different ways encouraged concern with the nature and identity of the Church, in the twentieth century it has been the ecumenical movement which has primarily contributed to an ever-growing interest in ecclesiology. Episcopally ordered and non-episcopally ordered churches have come to see that all churches in one way or another exercise *episcopé*, just as all churches have a *magisterium* or doctrinal teaching authority in some form or other whether or not that word is used. The close link between worship and ecclesiology can be seen in writers like de Lubac and Zizioulas, in which the Eucharist is definitive, and in the inspirational ecclesiologies of charismatic and Pentecostal churches. An increasingly secular Western world is the context of much ecumenical endeavour, as is also the rapid growth of churches in Africa and Asia and the encounter between Christianity and other faiths. All of these raise questions of Christian identity and the relation of faith and culture, just as the traditional theological language in which ecclesiology has been discussed has to engage with the different interpretations of the nature of religious belonging coming from disciplines such as sociology and anthropology.

The time is surely therefore ripe for a journal specifically devoted to ecclesiological matters to provide an academic forum for the discussion of these important issues. The *International Journal for the Study of the Christian Church* has been inaugurated with this in mind.

It is appropriate that this first issue should be one marking the bicentenary of the birth of John Henry Newman (1801–90) for a number of reasons. First there can be little doubt of the significance of Newman as a theologian, whose writing has continued to inform not only Roman Catholic theology but much more widely. Secondly, Newman's personal pilgrimage from his early Evangelical roots to his death as a Cardinal of the Roman Catholic Church inevitably meant that the doctrine of the Church was always fundamental to his concern. It is no accident that it was Newman who in 1838 first gave the word 'Anglicanism' its current provenance and identity, even though *ecclesia anglicana* has more ancient roots.[5] Believing that Christianity was a revealed religion and shaped by his study of the

---

[4] Cited in T. E. Yates, *Venn and Victorian Bishops abroad* (Studia Missionalia Upsalliensia, XXXIII) (Uppsala, 1978), p. 99.

[5] See the discussion in Stephen Sykes and John Booty (eds), *The Study of Anglicanism* (London and Philadelphia: SPCK/Fortress Press, 1988), pp. 406–7, 424.

Fathers and then the seventeenth-century Anglican divines in his *Lectures on the Prophetical Office of the Church* (1837) Newman endeavoured to give a systematic exposition to the *via media* of Anglicanism, engaging on the one hand with a *sola scriptura* Protestantism, and on the other with a Roman Catholic Church which he believed had added to the faith. The touchstone was, as it had often been for the Anglican seventeenth-century divines, 'antiquity' – the consensus of the Fathers of the Church. The problem was how such an historical touchstone could cope with the fact of change – a question which for Newman was to lead him to the conclusion that, if Christianity were a revealed religion, and intended for all time, it must needs have an infallible expounder – a thesis set out with careful considera-tion in his 1845 *Essay on the Development of Christian Doctrine*. Change there must necessarily be, but change on principle, and principle conserving the *depositum* of faith, the 'faith once committed to the saints'. Vincent of Lérins in his *Commonitoria* (434), as Newman was well aware, appealed to universality, antiquity, and consent but did not rule out development, maintaining that if the seed sown was wheat, it was wheat that should grow from it.

> Though a certain clarity of form may have been added, still the same nature of each type remains. God forbid that those fields of roses which are the Catholic mind be turned into a jungle of thorns and thistles. God forbid that in this spiritual paradise, there come forth darnel and aconite from the branches of cinnamon and balsam.[6]

From his reading of scripture, the Fathers and the Anglican divines Newman developed a strong sense of the catholic *ethos* as marking the catholic identity of the Church. It was a word to which, although derived from Aristotle, John Keble had given currency as describing a quality of mind and manners. As Keble's biographer, J. T. Coleridge, put it, referring to Keble's understanding of the character of formation offered by the Oxford of his early experience: 'it imported certainly no intellectual quality, scarcely even any distinct moral one, but an habitual toning, or colouring, diffused over all a man's moral qualities, giving the exercise of them a peculiar gentleness or grace'.[7] It might be said in certain respects to approxi-mate to something of what is conveyed by uses of the word 'spirituality' today. When Newman wrote in 1835 to Sir James Stephen that 'Christians

---

[6] Vincent of Lérins, *Commonitoria*, I.23.

[7] J. T. Coleridge, *A Memoir of the Rev. John Keble, M.A. late Vicar of Hursley* (Oxford and London: James Parker & Co., 1874), pp. 398–9. Cf. the comments by Stephen Prickett in his essay on John Keble in Geoffrey Rowell (ed.), *The English Religious Tradition and the Genius of Anglicanism* (Wantage: IKON, 1992), p. 203.

receive the Gospel literally on their knees, and in a temper altogether different from that critical and argumentative spirit which sitting and listening engender', he urged that Christian truth was taught by rites and ceremonies. 'No mode of teaching can be imagined so public, constant, impressive, permanent, and at the same time reverential than that which makes the forms of devotion the memorial and declaration of doctrine – reverential because the very posture of the mind in worship is necessarily such.'[8] The Church was a worshipping community, and Christian truth, which was the truth of God, could only be apprehended by a mind and heart that were responsive in a total way to the God who was the source of the mystery of their being. For Newman revelation and mystery went hand in hand, and credal statements, however just and true they were, always pointed beyond themselves to the mystery of God. So he put in his last University Sermon on the Development of Doctrine:

> Creeds and dogmas live in the one idea which they are designed to express, and which alone is substantive; and are necessary only because the human mind cannot reflect upon that idea, except piecemeal, cannot use it in its oneness and entireness, nor without resolving it into a series of aspects and relations. And in matter of fact these expressions are never equivalent to it; we are able, indeed, to define the creations of our own minds, for they are what we make them and nothing else; but it were as easy to create what is real as to define it; and thus the Catholic dogmas are, after all, but symbols of a Divine fact, which, far from being compassed by those very propositions, would not be exhausted, nor fathomed, by a thousand.[9]

In the same vein Newman's understanding of tradition was concerned to set the formal definitions of creeds and councils (the episcopal tradition) in the context of the much broader 'prophetic tradition', which recognised the informal ways in which faith is affirmed and handed on – that 'certain body of Truth, pervading the Church like an atmosphere, irregular in shape from its very profusion and exuberance; at times separable only in idea from Episcopal Tradition . . .; partly written, partly the interpretation of Scripture, partly preserved in intellectual expressions, partly latent in the spirit and temper of Christians; poured to and fro in closets and upon the housetops, in liturgies, in controversial works, in obscure fragments, in sermons, in popular prejudices, in local customs'.[10]

[8] Thomas Gornall, SJ (ed.), *The Letters and Diaries of John Henry Newman* (Oxford: Clarendon Press, 1981), p. 46; J. H. Newman to Sir James Stephen, 16 March 1835.

[9] J. H. Newman, *Fifteen Sermons preached before the University of Oxford* (London: Longmans, Green & Co., 3rd edn, 1898), pp. 331–2.

[10] J. H. Newman, *The Via Media of the Anglican Church* (H. D. Weidner (ed.)) (Oxford: Clarendon Press, 1990), p. 268.

If Newman was aware of the complex character of tradition and Christian continuity he was similarly aware of the complexities of the relationship of faith and reason, explored first of all in his Oxford University Sermons, but definitively in *The Grammar of Assent*. Important aspects of the relationship between all of these are drawn out in David Brown's contribution to this first and special issue of the *Journal* on the theme of '*Phronesis*, Development and Doctrinal Definition'. The other contributions underline other important aspects of Newman's ecclesiology and of its development.

Bishop Philip Boyce's exploration into holiness as a mark of the Church in Newman's writings is a reminder that the twin and almost coincidental events of the episcopal attacks on *Tract 90* and the perceived undermining of a catholic understanding of Anglicanism as a result of the Anglo-Prussian scheme for the Jerusalem bishopric, led Newman to fall back on the note of holiness as evidence for the catholicity of Anglicanism.[11] But the call to holiness was always central in Newman's understanding of the Christian life, as the title of the first sermon in the *Parochial and Plain Sermons* makes clear; 'Holiness necessary for future blessedness'.[12] In a careful study of Newman's early ecclesiology Paul Vaiss shows how, as early as 1827, Newman had come to hold a sacramental view of the Church and its role and examines the evidence for the changes and development in Newman's understanding of the Church in the pre-Oxford Movement years, noting how the language of 'branches' of the 'holy Apostolic Church' entered Newman's vocabulary at the end of 1826. That sense of national expressions of the one church led to the original use of the term 'Anglo-Catholic' by both Newman and his fellow Tractarians, as witnessed in their gathering of the writings of major seventeenth-century Anglican theologians in *The Library of Anglo-Catholic Theology*. Newman's classical education, and then his reading of Justin's *Apologies*, Clement of Alexandria and Origen, led him to an understanding of the 'dispensation of paganism' in which, as he says in the *Apologia*, 'pagan literature, philosophy, and mythology, properly understood, were but a preparation for the Gospel. The Greek poets and sages were in a certain sense prophets . . . There had been a directly divine dispensation granted to the Jews; but there had been in some sense a dispensation carried on in favour

---

[11] The latest volume of Newman's *Letters and Diaries* (Volume VIII, Gerard Tracey (ed.), Oxford: Clarendon Press, 1999) makes it clear that it was the Jerusalem Bishopric affair that was the more disturbing to Newman, though the two issues became inter-twined.

[12] J. H. Newman, *Parochial and Plain Sermons*, I (London, Oxford and Cambridge: Rivingtons, 1875), pp. 1–14. The sermon was preached on the text 'Holiness, without which no man shall see the Lord' (Hebrews xii.14).

of the Gentiles'.[13] Once he had discovered this, it became an enduring element in his Christian understanding, as Francis McGrath demonstrates, noting how at the very end of his life he was able to welcome in this perspective a positive assessment of 'The Sacred Books of the East'.

Halbert Weidner develops the theme of Newman's 1877 Preface to the re-issue of his Anglican *Lectures on the Prophetical Office of the Church* as *The Via Media of the Anglican Church*, noting how Newman's sense of the balancing of the devotional, the prophetic (theological teaching), and 'kingly' (political institutional) offices of the Church, is drawn from his sense that the Church shared in the offices of Christ as prophet, priest and king.[14] Weidner develops this in the wider context of the search for a reformed Catholicism, but it is arguable that Newman's sense of *via media* is still to the fore in his concern to see an ecclesiology which not only balances the three offices, but avoids distortions within each of them. James Pereiro expounds in a challenging way the ecclesiological issues between Manning and Newman with reference to contemporary debate about the nature and identity of the Church and the place in Roman Catholic theology of 'ecclesial communities' – an issue raised sharply by the publication of *Dominus Jesus* by the Vatican Congregation for the Doctrine of the Faith in August 2000. For Manning the Holy Spirit was of prime importance in his understanding of the Church and Christian life, as is demonstrated by his published Anglican sermons. It was not for nothing that it was the Gorham Judgement's repudiation of the necessity of belief in baptismal regeneration (a doctrine affirming the gift of the Spirit in baptism, and hence the Spirit as the shaper of the Christian life from that moment) which was the final catalyst in Manning's move from the Church of England to the Church of Rome, and the same concern about the Spirit's providential directing of the Church was evident in Manning's strong advocacy of Papal Infallibility at Vatican I in 1870.

The ecclesiological issues with which Newman was so centrally concerned in his lifetime both as an Anglican and as a Roman Catholic are well illustrated by the contributors to this first and special issue of the *Journal*. They are issues that are still the concerns of the Church today in the context of inter-church relations and ecumenical agreements; in the issues of doctrinal change and development and the questions of church order and what counts as a Christian life-style; in the broad questions of Christian identity and contemporary culture; and the recurring theme of authority in the Church, the interpretation of scripture and the character

[13] J. H. Newman, *Apologia pro vita sua* (London: Longman, &c., 1864), p. 89.
[14] A theme, as Weidner notes, found in Pearson's *Exposition of the Creed* (1659).

of tradition, seen as constraint from the past or dynamic for the future. It is our hope that this new forum for discussion will enable Christians of all traditions to engage with some of these major issues, and to learn from those who have wrestled with them in the past, of which John Henry Newman is surely an outstanding example from whom we may profitably learn.

Newman's Ecclesiology in his Pre-Oxford Movement Years: A Historical and a Critical View

PAUL VAISS

NEWMAN's ecclesiology in the pre-Oxford Movement period can best be determined by a close examination of his sermon manuscripts. Since he generally destroyed them when his sermons were published, only the unpublished ones will fall within the scope of this study. The reason why such a work is necessary will become clear when one realises that, whenever Newman re-preached a sermon – and he did so very often – or prepared it for publication, he altered it significantly, sometimes rewriting the sermon completely. Thus, the surest means to trace his opinions at a given time is to resort to the manuscripts of his unpublished sermons.

My aim in this paper is first to delineate Newman's understanding of the Church, selecting a few significant themes as they unfold and evolve throughout the nine years between the time of his curacy at St Clement's (July 1824–February 1826) and his Mediterranean voyage (starting in December 1833). Some passages in his correspondence and occasional biographical material will shed some light on his spiritual development, on his doubts and hesitations, and on various elements. Finally, the critical appraisal of Newman's contradictions and difficulties at this period of his life will enable us to understand in what state of mind he was to launch the Oxford Movement and give us hints of why he eventually joined the Church of Rome.

Newman's ecclesiology: a thematic approach

When Newman took up his duties at St Clement's he was firmly grounded in the doctrines taught by the Evangelical wing of the Church of England.

Ecclesiology was certainly not a priority for Evangelicals; they rather privileged soteriology and, especially, the atonement. The second emphasis was sanctification, the third: missions, and ecclesiology was generally left far behind, so much so that, when faced with the issue of associating with the dissenters to promote the gospel of salvation in Christ, many set aside loyalty to their Church and some even ignored the opposition of their vicars or bishops; Wesley's and Whitefield's were no exceptional cases. Newman never went to those lengths but his first sermons are clearly centred on the atonement-justification as understood by the Evangelicals with very little space devoted to the Church, the Christian ministry or even the liturgy and the sacraments. This observation is essential, for as my concern will be to discuss Newman's ecclesiology at that time, one may easily feel the subject was prominent in his sermons and represented one of his priorities. It only acquired such a status at the outset of the following decade in 1830–1 and afterwards. Even then, there were strong 'Evangelical' periods in his life when his emphasis was on salvation and sanctification alternating with what, for lack of a better formula, I would call 'High Church' periods, when his emphasis was on the Church of England, its apostolic character, its threefold ministry, the means of grace it dispenses, its authority for teaching Christian doctrine, the sin of schism, etc.

The issue of infant baptism

Until the days when the action of Newman and his followers alienated the Evangelicals from the Oxford Movement – in 1835–6 and even more so after 1838 – baptism was not an issue with churchmen. They all believed that, according to the Anglican liturgy, baptism bestowed the gift of regeneration on the newly born baby and made him or her a member of Christ's Church. Yet, the Evangelicals would add that a definite conversion was necessary for the child to become a *real* Christian, whereas other Anglicans, especially those belonging to the High Church current, were averse to making genuine religion depend on what was to them an emotive experience. In the late 1830s the issue became the dividing line between two opposite factions, the animosity reaching its climax with the Gorham case (1848–50).[1] Then, one could distinguish between most Evangelicals who denied baptism any regenerative power, transferring it entirely to conversion, and the High Church party who believed that full regeneration was bestowed in baptism.

---

[1] Phillpotts, bishop of Exeter, had refused to accept a vicar called Gorham in his diocese because he denied infant baptism any regenerative power. Phillpotts considered him a heretic.

In a sermon preached in June 1824, we read:

Such characters however – who, so far from *waiting* on the Lord scarcely even *think* about Him and whose religious profession (such as it is) is adapted to *quiet* their consciences, rather than *from the fervent* desires of a contrite and renewed mind – characters of this pitiable description it is not intended should occupy our attention at present.[2]

When he re-preached the same sermon in October 1826, Newman amended it as follows:

The greater part indeed of professed Christians, so far from *waiting* on the Lord, scarcely even *think* about Him and their religious profession (such as it is) is adapted to quiet their conscience or *inflate* them with self-righteousness, rather than to satisfy the desires of a renewed mind – For these it is the duty of every good Christian to pray.

The differences between the two categories of people in the first version of the sermon is that the former are hardly Christians, they profess a deceptive religion, they haven't been renewed in their minds for they have not experienced 'contrition unto salvation', i.e. conversion. In the 1826 version, all 'professed Christians' are supposed to have 'the renewed mind' regeneration – although one category among them is indifferent to things religious. One can understand that behind the two versions of this sermon are different notions of regeneration and the efficacy of baptism.

Another of the early sermons seems to limit the Church to the converts and to consider them as the only regenerate:

'Believe on the Lord Jesus and thou shalt be saved' (Acts 16) – were you laden with ten thousand sins, His merits are sufficient to wash them all away. Only have faith in Him, and you are of that little flock to whom it is the Father's good pleasure to give the kingdom – Only have faith and you are the child of God (Gal. 3) in Christ Jesus by the power of the Holy Ghost.[3]

Yet, it would be hazardous to conclude that in 1824 Newman consistently considered only converted Christians as members of the Church of Christ. Actually, a few quotations from his sermons of that year are illuminating and puzzling as well:

We are at present members of the vine of God – we have been baptised into His Church, and are members of His visible communion.[4]

---

[2] Sermon 2 preached 23 June 1824 – Birmingham Oratory Papers [BO]: A 17–1 *St Clement's and later.*

[3] Sermon 27 preached 24 October 1824 – BO : A 17–1.

[4] Sermon 13 preached 22 August 1824 – BO : A 17–1.

The human heart is naturally selfish and most men remain in the same coldness and selfishness with which they were born. In vain have they been received into the Church by the waters of baptism.[5]

We have enjoyed the blessing of being early admitted by baptism into the Christian Church.[6]

Many are offered the gospel, many admitted into His visible Church, but few show themselves God's chosen servants by faith and holy living.[7]

At first sight, his position does not seem to have changed significantly when he came under High Church influences. In January 1826, he called on parents of baptised children 'to see that the grace given them as members of the Church be not bestowed in vain'.[8] A sermon of June 1828 asks the question:

Who are members of His Church? [. . .]. I answer, all children of Christian parents [. . .]. No question then seems to remain except about the time *when* justification takes place [. . .]. He has appointed a time – and that is *the time of baptism*.[9]

This passage seems to go a stage further by stating that even justification takes place at baptism. We may also notice that the later mentions of baptism as the rite that introduces into the Church do not refer explicitly to the 'visible Church'.

The visible Church versus the invisible Church

With these texts we are introduced into one of the subtleties of Evangelicalism:[10] the fundamental distinction drawn between the visible Church, which includes all the baptised, and the invisible Church, whose membership is restricted to Christ's true disciples – those who have experienced a genuine conversion. In a sermon of October 1824 we read:

We are planted in the inclosed vineyard of God's Church [. . .]. And so it is with the visible Church – it seems to abound in piety, charity and good works, but on looking close we find that this day of outward prosperity has corrupted it [. . .]. Alas, on too many the vinedresser (Gal. 4) bestows his labour in vain – they die unrepentant and unforgiven [. . .]. You must, in the words of our Church, beseech God 'to grant us true repentance and His Holy Spirit'.[11]

---

[5] Sermon 20 preached 12 September 1824 – BO : A 17–1.
[6] Sermon 22 preached 19 September 1824 – BO : B 3 – Box IV *Practical*.
[7] Sermon 16 preached 7 November 1824 – BO : A 17–1.
[8] Sermon 128 preached 8 January 1826 – BO : B 3 – Box IV *General Theology*.
[9] Sermon 169 preached 22 June 1828 – BO : A 50–3 *Mostly on the sacraments and the liturgy*.
[10] In fact the theory was first propounded by Calvin's early followers.
[11] Sermon 28 preached 17 October 1824 – BO : A 17–1.

An early sermon re-written in December 1828 apparently states a contrary opinion:

> Blessed be God, we do not live in a country partially within the Christian covenant, when relations and friends by nature are not by grace connected [. . .]. In our happy case, brethren by birth and brethren in the gospel – not only of the same blood but born again of the same gracious Spirit.[12]

Yet, a few months before, he had addressed his congregation in such a way as to force us to reconsider what might have been a hasty judgement.

> My brethren, I have said you are all, all whom I address, members of one body, the body of Christ [. . .]. Whether you are personally walking in the path of life, is a secret from the general Church we can but guess at [. . .]. Deceive not yourself now by hoping to be saved by present privileges – general privileges, unless converted into personal graces become witnesses against your souls [. . .]. To know for yourselves whether you really are Christians, you must retire into a secret chamber [. . .]; you must examine whether you are drawn on by the fear and love of God to seek after holiness [. . .]. These are some of the evidences of a renewed heart.[13]

Clearly Newman, preaching from the pulpit of St Mary's in 1828, is still an Evangelical who believes in the distinction between a visible Christian communion and the much more precious reality of a Church of saints, the select body of those whose salvation is assured. The gate one has to go through in order to step from the 'general Church' into the real Church, from 'general privileges' to the privileges of salvation and a 'renewed heart' is conversion. All the same, in November 1829, he clearly states that all the baptised are part of a 'visible society', a phrase he uses without lending it a negative connotation:

> He himself instituted a rite of incorporation into the visible society of his followers, and He dignified this rite and secured its perpetuity by making it a sacrament conveying a promise of grace [. . .]. He made that body a visible society by the sacrament of baptism.[14]

It seems then that towards the end of 1829, Newman had finally shed his lingering Evangelical notions of the Church with their subtle distinctions between a visible Church and the invisible company of the 'true Christians', the regenerate body of the elect. But nothing is simple when one is confronted with Newman's spiritual itinerary. In a sermon he

---

[12] Sermon 114 re-written for 25 December 1828 – BO : B 3 – Box IV *General Theology*.

[13] Sermon 120 re-written for 27 April 1828 – BO : A 50–2 *Some, on the doctrine of the Church*.

[14] Sermon 216 preached 15 November 1829 – BO : A 50–2.

preached in October 1830 – and repeated in 1833, 1838 and in 1841 – we read:

> Hid are his saints – we cannot pick them out from the world – here and there only as we come near them and closely we tell them in their mortal disguise (Luke 24) by the burning of our own hearts within us – but sure we are, and may take comfort from the thought, that on all sides of us there are many scattered, above and below, who hear Christ's voice and follow Him.[15]

Such language is unmistakably Evangelical; it distinguishes in the visible multitude of Christians a company of saints, those who truly follow Christ, who are different from the rest of the world although it is very difficult to single them out. Christopher Dawson has observed that Newman's emphasis was not so much on 'the hierarchical principle of the episcopal succession than on the more mystical notion of an apostolical succession of saints'.[16] It is to this 'little flock' that Newman refers a little later:

> Whether a Christian teacher preach but half the gospel, or the whole gospel, or the gospel complied with much more besides, still anyhow the true sheep of Christ will hear Christ's voice amid his teaching and follow Christ, they will separate the wheat from the chaff.[17]

It is exactly the same view that he expresses in his most famous university sermon 'Personal Influence the Means of Propagating the Truth' which he delivered in 1832:

> In all ages true Christians, though contained in [the Church], and forming its life and strength, are scattered and hidden in the multitude, and, but partially recognizing each other, have no means of combining and co-operating.[18]

He continues along the same line, observing:

> And if such be the personal influence exerted by the Teacher of Truth over the mixed crowd of men whom he encounters, what will be His power over that select number, just referred to, who have already, in a measure, disciplined their hearts after the law of holiness [. . .]. These are they whom the Lord especially calls His 'elect', and came to 'gather in one' for they are worthy.[19]

Newman's typically Evangelical vision of the Church is here drawn to its most radical consequences, i.e. the Church of Christ is exclusively

---

[15] Sermon 261 preached 18 October 1830 – BO : A 17–1.

[16] Christopher Dawson, *The Spirit of the Oxford Movement* (London, 1933), p. 41.

[17] Sermon 290 preached 20 March 1831 – BO : A 50–5 *Personal*.

[18] J. H. Newman, *Fifteen Sermons preached before the University of Oxford* (Westminster, MD: Christian Classics, 1966), Sermon V, p. 77. The sermon was preached on 22 January 1832.

[19] Ibid., p. 95.

composed of converts. This is the position that was taken by those who eventually seceded from the Church of England to join the dissenters.[20] On 21 October 1832, he was still insisting that:

> To have the full privileges of the gospel, to be acknowledged as the true sons of God, His true elect, His saints in whom He delighteth [. . .] we must be consistent and confirmed believers [. . .] and converted in the nature of our souls from sin to holiness [. . .].[21]

Is the Church of England Protestant or Catholic?

It may appear awkward to state the issue in such terms, yet Newman's perception of his Church was to depend on the answers he could give to this question. In one of his early sermons he declared: 'We have been born in the Protestant Church', a statement which he altered into 'We have been born into the true Church' when he re-preached it in 1835.[22] In January 1826, Newman gave a more complete view of his position:

> If we compare the Romish or the Greek Church with our own we shall find many ceremonies and rites different from ours – Doubtless we also differ from them in many essential matters, still it is quite true that great parts of our disagreement are merely outward – The case is the same if we compare our Church with the Scotch or again the Lutheran Church in Germany. A great part of the difference is in indifferent matters in which all may be right.[23]

So far, all Christian Churches are recognised as being close to the Church of England, especially the Protestant Churches. At the end of that year, a new phrase entered Newman's vocabulary:

> And this our Holy Apostolic Church [. . .] exists even to this day – one branch of it derived from the apostles is in this country – another (as we trust) in Scotland – in France another – in Spain, Greece, Rome other branches – all members and descendants of that primitive Church for which the Apostles laid down their lives [. . .]. We alas ourselves were once corrupted as some of them are still but God has visited us with the spirit of reformation and we trust that in His good time He will visit them too.[24]

---

[20] On this subject, see my 'Newman's state of mind on the eve of his Italian tour' in Paul Vaiss (ed.), *From Oxford to the People* (Leominster: Gracewing, 1996), especially pp. 211–12.

[21] Sermon 343 preached 21 October 1832 – BO : B 3 Box IV *General Theology*.

[22] Sermon 22 (see note 6).

[23] Sermon 130 preached 15 January 1826 – BO : A 50–1 *On General Theology*.

[24] Sermon 157 preached 19 November 1826 – BO : A 50–2 *Some, on the doctrine of the Church*.

It is clear that Newman, who has discovered the apostolic character of the Church of England, extends it to the Presbyterian Church of Scotland, to the Lutheran, the Orthodox, and the Roman Churches, each being considered as a branch of the universal Church. The Reformation is presented as a positive event, not yet as a mixed blessing. The same appreciative assessment can be found in a sermon of July 1828 that has to do with the Eucharist:

> Some centuries ago, when our Church, and christendom in general, had become gradually corrupted in the long course of years, the uses and purposes of Holy Communion were altogether perverted [. . .]. After the reformation then (as it is called) i.e. when our Church returned to the simplicity of the primitive times and laid aside those human additions with which its doctrines and discipline were burdened and deformed [. . .].[25]

Later sermons show that Newman gradually began to distinguish between the Episcopal Churches that had preserved the apostolic succession and could be considered branches of the one Apostolic and Catholic Church [the Churches of England, of Rome and those of the East] and the others. It is perceptible in a sermon of November 1829:

> Much as the Church of Christ has erred, in this she has kept the faith – she has always enforced the duty of obedience to the Apostolic rule of order (indeed her existence depended on it) – and to this day that very Church which Apostles planted remains vested in the successors of the Apostles throughout the Christian world – Though there are and ever have been separatists from the Church and small parties, yet the general body of Christians throughout the world are and ever have been branches from the Church of Jerusalem – and their ministers, not self-appointed teachers, but ordained in regular unbroken succession from the Apostles.[26]

A further step away from the Protestant Churches is taken before the following year is over. In November 1830 he declares:

> One thousand and seven hundred years are gone, and still the same society which the Apostles once set up, remains throughout the world in its several branches. It has never been dissolved, never been refounded [. . .]. Our own branch descended from the Roman Church a thousand years since, still declares the glory of God and His handiwork, responding to those chants of praise which the East and South pour forth. Nor is there in those branches of the one Christian body, nor has there been for any time, error or corruption of faith, sufficient to impair its authority [. . .]. For doubtless the Catholic Church

[25] Sermon 172 preached 19 July 1828 – BO : A 50–3 *Mostly on the sacraments and Liturgy.*

[26] Sermon 216 preached 15 November 1829 – BO : A 50–2.

of which we are part is so far preferable to other Christian bodies [. . .] chiefly because its doctrine and discipline form a much higher and nobler Christian character than any other religious system.[27]

The necessity of the Reformation seems not merely to be downplayed, but altogether denied. The differences between the Church of England and Rome appear not too serious but the chasm between the Apostolic Churches [Rome, Constantinople and Canterbury] and the dissenters is formidable. This impression is confirmed by a sermon of December 1831 in which we read:

> Can we point to the age in former days when the lineally descended Apostolic Church did not teach the fundamentals of faith whatever might be its incidental corruptions? Can we point to a time in which its corruptions were comparatively greater than any other antagonist system?[28]

I have shown elsewhere that Newman's religious opinions before the Oxford Movement began varied considerably.[29] There were periods when he reverted to his early Evangelical beliefs and completely left out of his sermons any form of High Church teaching. The last of those periods extended throughout the year 1832. As far as his ecclesiology is concerned, this does not necessarily mean that he changed his views whenever he entered an Evangelical stage of his life. It simply means that other aspects of Christian doctrine took precedence, ecclesiological matters being left in abeyance. All the same, knowing this characteristic of his spiritual itinerary, one would tend to be very cautious and abstain from asserting that Newman's understanding of the Church consistently evolved, stage after stage, from a Protestant Evangelical view to a radically High Church conception. An uninformed study of the successive alterations of a phrase in sermon 120, for instance, may lead to hazardous conclusions. In the original text he wrote: 'Why have we not always before our eyes the good of the Church?'. When he revised it a year or two later he emended it into 'the good of the universal Church' and in a second revision he wrote 'the Catholic Apostolic Church'.[30]

---

[27] Sermon 270 preached 28 November 1830 – BO : A 50–2.

[28] Sermon 323 preached 18 December 1831 – BO : A 50–2.

[29] See my book *Newman, sa vie, sa pensée et sa spiritualité* (Paris: L'Harmattan, 1991). In a condensed form there is my contribution to *From Oxford to the People*, op. cit. and my article 'Les sermons de Newman de 1829 à 1832: reflets de sa perplexité', in *Études Newmaniennes* 17 – 2001.

[30] The sermon was first preached on 27 November 1825, then on 10 September 1826, on 26 August 1827, on 27 March 1828 and then in 1831 and in 1841.

The Church of England, an Established Church

On this subject, a quotation from a late sermon will suffice, since Newman never used the pulpit in those days to voice his misgivings as to the interference of the State in matters of Church government, discipline and doctrine.

> It is the privilege of this country to be a Christian country, and the only means of preserving it so, is to place the Church, which is the channel of the Christian blessings, in a prominent place. In St Barnabas' day, this was done by miraculous agency – since that is withdrawn it must be effected by temporal privileges. We maintain the Church as we do any other institution or power – our kin and noblemen have power through their wealth and authority, and the Church must have it in the same way. This led our ancestors (who are ever to be revered for it) to make large grants of property to the Church – to induce its ministers into the high places of trust and power.[31]

The Church as the mediator of God's grace

One of the main characteristics of Evangelicalism was its tendency to minimise the sacramental aspects of the Christian ordinances and the liturgy and to give the sermon precedence over the latter. Yet, as early as 1827, Newman seems to have adopted a sacramental view of the Church and of its role. In a sermon written in August of that year, he declares:

> [Christ] has founded a Church, with whom He has lodged both grace and teaching – to the Church of Christ belong the means of grace such as the sacraments, ordinances, and the weekly worship of God [. . .]. The Catholic Church of God then, is [. . .] the guardian and expounder of the Word of God, and the minister of His Spirit.[32]

In September 1828, Newman insists on the role of the Church:

> The Christian Church itself is one most important mediator between God and the world [. . .]. It receives the gifts of the Spirit of God, and by sacraments and ordinances, by prayers, by preaching, by the establishment of education, it conveys the gospel to the world at large.[33]

A sermon of March 1829 states that 'the Bible contains the *matter* out of which the Church forms the Christian doctrines – the Church is the guardian, expounder and dispenser of Scripture'.[34] This unevangelical view

---

[31] Sermon 302 preached 11 June 1831 – BO : A 17–1 *St Clement's and later.*
[32] Sermon 162 preached 19 August 1827 – BO : B3 Box IV *General Theology.*
[33] Sermon 176 preached 14 September 1828 – BO : B3 Box IV *The Mediator.*
[34] Sermon 191 preached 22 March 1829 – BO : A 50–5 *Personal.*

reflects Hawkins' contention – which he expounded in a sermon of 1819 'On the Use and Importance of Unauthoritative Tradition' – that 'the sacred text was never intended to teach doctrine but only to prove it, and that, if we would learn doctrine, we must have recourse to the formularies of the Church'.[35] Only seven months later, Newman gives the Church an even more exalted position: 'Christ did not promise to give us grace immediately from Himself, but through His Holy Spirit, and that Holy Spirit has taken up his abode in His Church'.[36] In a sermon of February 1830, he goes somewhat further:

> But [Christ] is gone – whom has He left to teach us in His stead and to remind us of Him? He has left His Church in which the Spirit dwells [. . .]. This society or Church supplies His place as a visible and present guide – This Church is the spiritual mother of us all and the Liturgy is her voice.[37]

It is no longer the Holy Spirit, as such, who has replaced Christ, it is His Church indwelt by the Spirit and, in that capacity, she is now viewed by Newman as being our 'present guide'. The role of the liturgy – the 'voice' of the Church – is further emphasised in this sermon:

> The same Spirit which inspired Scripture is still with the Church and lives within Christ's true servants and such composed the Church services. In the prayers of the Liturgy we have the Scriptures digested and commented by those whose hearts the Holy Ghost had cleansed and made His temple.

The liturgy is given an even more exalted role in a sermon preached in March 1831:

> Men in this day speak as if hearing what they call preaching was *the* great reason of their coming hither, whereas the great duty, the expressly enjoined duty, and the richly privileged duty is *communion* and prayer [. . .]. Preaching will benefit those who do seek Him, but it will not commonly create a heart to seek Him, when it does not exist. Nothing can move us to holiness but God's grace and our will cooperating with it and God's grace is promised not through preaching, but through the Sacraments and through whatever has a sacramental character, and public prayer is of this kind.[38]

The offices of priests and bishops

Newman very early had a lofty notion of the ministry. In a sermon of 1826, we read:

[35] J. H. Newman, *Apologia Pro Vita Sua* (New York: Norton edition, 1968), pp. 20–1.

[36] Sermon 213 preached 25 October 1829 – BO : A 17–1.

[37] Sermon 225 preached 7 February 1830 – BO : A 50–3 *Mostly on the sacraments and Liturgy.*

[38] Sermon 290 (see note 17).

Ambassadors of Christ are above the censures or the praises of men – they are invested in a character above their own – and are amenable to none but their spiritual Head. To them is delegated the office once given to Levi – they are to teach God's judgements and declare His law – and He will graciously bless their labour and accept the work of their hands and smite with spiritual punishment those who rise up against them.[39]

At an ordination service held at Christ Church Cathedral, Oxford, in 1831 he described the ministerial office in solemn words:

The ministerial body, the ecclesiastical polity, has, it is plain, a venerable character and a dignity, to which no other body can lay claim – It is without parallel in the world, viewed as an historical fact – With what feelings of exultation and at once of conscious unworthiness do we contemplate our admission to any celebrated society framed for whatever object – much more is it an honour to incorporate members of that blessed company of Christian members of the apostolic body.[40]

He goes on to underline the office of Christian priests as the dispensers of the sacraments:

Lastly let us reflect upon the peculiar blessedness of those privileges of which this body is the guardian and channel. I need not recount what the Christian blessings are, nor how greatly they surpass any other conceivable blessing – yet they are derived to the multitude of believers through the sacraments alone as means greatly necessary – and the sacraments are administered solely by the ministerial order.

He had already referred to this office in the first sermon of a series on the liturgy in 1830:

When [a Christian minister] prays as the voice of the congregation (and much more when he celebrates the two sacraments) he is like Christ exalted, presenting redeemed sinners to the Father and granting the gifts of grace. When he teaches, he executes almost a Deacon's office; when he prays a Priest's.[41]

The episcopal order and the issue of its discontinuance in some Protestant Churches receive little attention. In a sermon of 1829, he declares:

They [the apostles] placed single Bishops in each separate church – Bishops are centres of unity, types of Christ mystical, the new spiritual man, witnesses of the purpose of Christ that we should be one in Him, protections against schism [. . .].[42]

[39] Sermon 150 preached 23 April 1826 – BO : A 17–1.
[40] Sermon 323 (see note 28).
[41] Sermon 224 preached 31 January 1830 – BO : A 50–3.
[42] Sermon 216 (see note 14).

Blaming those who reject all form of Church government, he continues:

> Indeed for 1500 years there was *no* difference on the question of Church government at all – what we and the greater number of Christian countries still maintain, the episcopal form, was universally received – and after that time when questions arose about it, still so far from being thought a point of significant importance, those who differed from us still considered sober continuance in *some* form or *other* a solemn duty.

His position is quite tolerant, there is no suggestion that the rejection of bishops in any way places the Protestant Churches concerned in an inferior position. On 21 March 1832, a day of national fast on the occasion of a cholera epidemic, Newman preached a solemn sermon in which he deplored the attitude of the Press:

> Consider merely how the notion of making this a day of humiliation was ridiculed, or at best coldly suffered by these publications [. . .]. Dwell for a moment on their profane mocking of our Holy Church, which the apostles founded, and of its rulers the Bishops, the successors of the apostles, who are to be honoured for their high office sake.[43]

This is the first mention of the apostolical succession that we find in Newman's sermons.

Some biographical elements

A sure indicator of Newman's ecclesiology in those years is his attitude to the Bible Society and the Church Missionary Society, both largely dominated by the Evangelicals and tolerating associations with the dissenters. On 29 May 1828, he addressed the Oxford branch of the Bible Society observing that:

> To belong to this Society is by many persons thought a strange inconsistency in a Churchman, as if he could not belong to it without a plain sacrifice of principle [. . .]. Now that there may be *objections* in a Churchman's mind to joining this Society may be readily allowed. I, for one, think there are strong and grave objections to his joining it [. . .]. There are also real objections *to keeping aloof*.[44]

So what are the objections a Churchman may have against this society?

> Suppose it is objected that the principle of the Bible Society creates a certain indifference to the preservation of Ecclesiastical Order, or that it encourages

---

[43] Sermon 332 preached 21 March 1832 – BO : B3 Box IV *General Theology*.

[44] *The Letters and Diaries of John Henry Newman*, [L.D.] (Oxford: Clarendon Press, 1979), vol. II, pp. 385–6.

the notion that the Bible may be rightly understood without the need of theological learning or a previous religious education. I may think these alleged effects of the institution *bad* – nay I may even allow that they in a degree exist – and yet in spite of them on the whole see cause to join the Society [. . .]. [A Churchman] may still think, as he ought to think, that the disunion of Christians in discipline and form of worship is a grievous evil [. . .] – but in cooperating with Christians of different denominations for the multiplication of copies of the Bible, he is not acting *inconsistently* with this his firm persuasion.[45]

Apparently, two years later, he had changed his mind since on 8 June 1830 he withdrew from the Bible Society.[46] He explained his decision in a letter to his friend Simeon Lloyd Pope:

I have always thought there were great evils in the Society – but I considered that by joining it you lessened them. The experience of some years has convinced me that you increase them. The tendency of the age is towards *liberalism* – i.e. a thinking established notions worth nothing – in this system a disregard of religion is included. No religion will survive if deprived of its forms. It is nothing to say *it is truth* – moral *truth* is not acceptable to man's heart; it must be enforced by authority of some kind or other. Miracles are a kind of authority [. . .] an ecclesiastical system, i.e. forms, another [. . .]. Miracles have ceased [. . .] whereas a system of Church government was *actually established* by the Apostles. And is thus the *legitimate* enforcement of Christian truth. The liberals know this – and are in every possible manner trying to break it up – and I think the B.S. (unconsciously) is a means of aiding their object. *Hence it is joined by liberals* [. . .].[47]

The main justification Newman gives highlights two aspects of his ecclesiology that were to play a major part in his religious development. The first is quite straightforward: the necessity to resist all forms of liberalism. The second is the need for an indisputable source of authority that renders the apostolicity of the Church of England so important.

After a series of disagreements and a strained relationship with the Evangelical leaders of the Oxford branch of the CMS, Newman wrote and distributed a pamphlet (in February 1830) condemning some practices of the society and, surprisingly enough when one has read the letter above, calling for a massive enrolment of conservative churchmen in the CMS to change it from the inside.

The facts of the case are these. A society for missionary purposes, supported mainly by members of the Church of England, professing her doctrines and

---

[45] Ibid.
[46] Ibid., p. 228.
[47] Ibid., pp. 264–5.

discipline, and making use of her name, has extended its operations into all the dioceses of the kingdom; and (as far as its object is concerned) has laid out anew the Church's territory, dividing it into districts of its own appointing. It has moreover remodelled our ecclesiastical system, the functions of which are brought under the supreme direction of a committee of management in London [. . .]. Moreover, its practice of addressing itself to the multitude in public meetings, – besides offending against the peculiar sobriety of our Church's character, – has a direct tendency to disarrange her parochial system; to give a prominence to preaching over other religious ordinances [. . .] and to make the people, not the Bishop, the basis and moving principle of her constitution.[48]

The charge of trespassing on parochial boundaries and setting up a parallel territorial division of the country recalls one of the most contentious subjects in the dispute between the Methodists and the Church authorities. Accusing the CMS of making 'the people, not the Bishop' its foundation and its decision-making organ is interesting, not only because Newman gives prominence to the bishops in Church government. It is also significant since it underlines his constant defiance of democracy and his insistence on an authoritarian form of government deriving its legitimacy from an apostolic fountainhead.

A critical view

Hardly a few months after his conversion of 1816, Newman was confronted by the incompatibility of his positions as an Evangelical and the liturgy of the Church of England. For, whereas the ritual of the service of baptism clearly declares that the new born baby is regenerated by the sacrament, Evangelical teaching insisted so much on regeneration as the outcome of a conversion experience that it practically emptied infant baptism of its meaning.[49] Of course, Newman was not alone to feel uneasy. The issue had been debated by Evangelicals long before and many unsatisfactory answers were offered.[50] So that, at first sight, it is not surprising that Newman should have varied in his opinions on the subject. Yet, when one compares his reactions to those of other Evangelicals such as William Wilberforce, Charles Simeon or John and Henry Venn, it becomes obvious that he was uncommonly sensitive to the difficulties of the case. As we saw, Newman's attitude to baptismal regeneration largely conditioned his view of the Church. Now, this first area of uncertainty lies at the core of his uneasy

---

[48] J. H. Newman, *The Via Media of the Anglican Church*, vol. II, p. 4 (London, 1877 edn).

[49] See my book [1991], op. cit., pp. 60–7.

[50] See, for example, the correspondence between Newman and Mayers over Beveridge – *L.D.*, vol. I, pp. 30–4.

relationship to Anglicanism. For anyone familiar with Newman's writings – be they private, as his letters and diaries, or public, as his sermons and numerous publications – the sense of a yearning after certainty and an intellectually consistent set of beliefs appears evident.[51] And the Church of England, as he perceived it, never gave him a durably satisfactory answer to his need. One could easily cite several issues over which he was embarrassed.

Another aspect that needs to be stressed, although it does not bear directly on our subject, is the tormented way in which his views evolved. As one reads the extracts from his sermons given in this paper, it seems that Newman's conception of the Church developed smoothly, gaining substance with time and becoming gradually more akin to traditional High Church notions. Yet, as I suggested before, things were not so simple. For almost all the passages in his sermons – not only those quoted here – that bear on ecclesiology are to be found at particular periods of his life and practically never at those when Evangelical themes came back in full force. I will mention those different periods which I have discussed elsewhere:[52]

- from January to April 1829: Evangelical themes only,
- from May 1829 to February 1830: High Church themes,
- from March to October 1830: predominantly Evangelical themes,
- from November 1830 to January 1832: High Church themes dominate,
- from January to November 1832: Evangelical themes exclusively.

These successive periods do not reflect necessarily clear-cut changes of views but they are, to say the least, revealing as to Newman's lack of certainty and tentative attempts at finding his way.

This brings us to yet another of Newman's preoccupations in his Anglican years. For Evangelicals, inside and outside of the Church of England, the Bible only was the source and foundation of authority. In this they felt they were simply rediscovering one of the key principles of the Reformation: 'sola Scriptura'. When Newman came under the influence of Whately and Hawkins,[53] and especially when he read the latter's sermon on tradition, he began to see new prospects opening up. For, as he grasped the notion of an ecclesiastical tradition complementing and interpreting the Bible, the nexus of authority was displaced towards the Church. There

[51] It is remarkable, in this respect, that his last published work should be An Essay in aid of a Grammar of Assent.

[52] See my book [1991], op. cit., pp. 308–28 and 397–400. See also my articles mentioned at note 29.

[53] They were the leading dons of the brilliant exceptionally open-minded group of Oriel College intellectuals.

he readily admitted the divinely sanctioned role and authority of bishops legitimised by the apostolical succession. Simultaneously, the sacred character of the Word of God was extended to the Church as a visible institution and, especially, to its leadership. When he began to question the apostolicity of his Church, i.e. the legitimacy of its authority, then the arguments in favour of the Church of Rome gained overwhelming strength.

The apparently artificial distinction Newman at times drew between a 'visible' and an 'invisible' Church was also part of a very real problem. It was simply one aspect of his questionings as to the real nature of the Church, a line of investigation that was to last well into his Roman Catholic period. Dawson's remark concerning Newman's view of the Church as an 'apostolical succession of saints'[54] harks back to his Evangelical days and may also have a bearing on his attitude concerning the consultation of the faithful in matters of doctrine which appeared so scandalous to the hierarchy.[55]

It is interesting to see that most of the themes of the *Tracts for the Times* are to be found in the sermons Newman preached over the nine years immediately preceding the Oxford Movement. Even more striking is the fact that we also find some of the most serious contradictions he would have to solve, sometimes at great cost. Some, such as Golightly or – for a short period – Newman's own brother Francis, drew closer to the Evangelicals. Others followed Newman in the Church of Rome. The majority remained in the Church of England with Keble or Pusey, and, doing so, they were not necessarily uneasy or resigned.

[54] See note 16.
[55] I allude here to the publication of the article bearing that title in the *Rambler* of July 1859 and its aftermath.

John Henry Newman and the Dispensation of Paganism

FRANCIS McGRATH

J OHN HENRY NEWMAN first used the term *Dispensation of Paganism*
in his second university sermon, 'The Influence of Natural and
Revealed Religion Respectively', preached on Easter Tuesday, 13 April
1830.[1] Towards the beginning of the sermon, he proposed that no
religious system anywhere had ever been established through unaided
reason. Although a mere fraction of the globe had been honoured with
an 'authenticated revelation' from God, no race of people had ever been
denied revelation of some sort. Classical literature is a fairly reliable
barometer of the actual religious state of pagan cultures and provides
evidence of a 'practical' creed in natural religion of which personal
conscience forms its 'essential principle and sanction'. Personal conscience
implies a relationship between an individual and a reality exterior and
superior to him or herself. It also implies an excellence which we do not
possess and points to an independent 'tribunal' over which we have no
control. And the more we obey this 'inward monitor', the 'clearer, the
more exalted, and the more varied its dictates become'. Personal conscience
supplies us with the basic building blocks of a religious system.[2]

---

[1] Importantly, the sermon prefigures in topic and order the great final Chapter X of the
Grammar of Assent. The tone of the latter, however, is guarded in the extreme, and this
almost certainly arises from the Roman Catholic theological climate of the time (1870),
rather than from a change of view. The absence of the term 'Dispensation of Paganism'
probably comes from a reluctance to use the *lingua franca* of Protestant apologetics. Though
the term 'dispensation' appears in the Douai-Rheims version of the New Testament, it only
appears in Catholic theological manuals and treatises as referring to different forms of
canonical exemption.

[2] *Fifteen Sermons preached before the University of Oxford*, U.S. II. 17–18. Newman went
on to remark that 'the inward law of Conscience brings with it no proof of its truth . . .
all obedience to it is of the nature of Faith' (ibid., p. 19). Newman later regretted the

Personal conscience is a constant reminder of what will happen in the next life if we behave badly in this one. It offers no proof of its authority; it commands attention and demands unyielding obedience. While conscience is the 'sanction' of natural religion, it can grow, when properly nurtured, into a personal code of conduct as well. A well-informed conscience 'habitually and honestly conforming itself to its own full sense of duty, will at length enjoin or forbid with an authority second only to an inspired oracle'. Even in heathen countries, well-informed consciences can spot the difference between right and wrong with a great deal of 'precision', and can 'elicit confirmation of its faith even out of the corruptions of the truth'.

Such a large, practical creed is attainable by any vigorous, God-fearing mind under the divine aegis of a Dispensation of Paganism. It is even conceivable that no 'essential character of Scripture doctrine . . . is without its place in this moral revelation'. Conscience provides insights into specific areas of morality to which human beings are 'instinctively drawn'. It warns of a 'judgement to come' for everyone and offers fleeting insights into God's infinite 'benevolence, wisdom, and power', as well as providing a set of basic moral laws which are universal. It also gives reassurance that forgiveness is possible and that we shall never go wrong if we follow its directions.[3]

Of themselves, such insights are a limited means to a limited end because they tell us very little about *who* the God of natural religion really is. Although awesome and powerful, this God remains an abstraction, never emerges as a God of love. But the Gospels, by telling simple stories about the life, death and resurrection of Jesus Christ, reveal this God of love and throw light on to some of the fundamental questions about the human condition and human destiny:

> The life of Christ brings together and concentrates truths concerning the chief good and the laws of our being, which wander idle and forlorn over the surface of the moral world, and often appear to diverge from each other. It collects the scattered rays of light, which, in the first days of creation, were poured over the whole face of nature, into certain intelligible centres, in the firmament of the heaven . . . Our Saviour has in Scripture all those abstract titles of moral excellence bestowed upon Him which philosophers have invented. He is the Word, the Light, the Life, the Truth, Wisdom, the Divine Glory.[4]

Newman's 1830 views on the existence of revelation outside the Christian and Jewish dispensations were, indeed, a far cry from the views

---

extravagance of expression, remarking that: 'The last sentence . . . needs modification. Simple obedience to Conscience is *not* Faith' (*Philosophical Notebook* II, 51).

[3] Ibid., pp. 20–1.

[4] Ibid., pp. 27–8.

expressed a few years earlier when, as curate of St Clement's Church in Oxford, he preached a series of ten rather wooden and contrived sermons on revelation in the weeks before Christmas 1825. Though fast acquiring full Noetic credentials by this time, he was still relying on evangelical sources, such as Daniel Wilson, future Anglican bishop of Calcutta, and the Scottish religious thinker, Thomas Erskine.[5] In spite of, or rather, because of their artificiality, the sermons are valuable for gauging *what* he then considered important and *how* he presented his arguments from a standpoint still hung with Evangelical totems and taboos. They are also a benchmark to measure the quantum leap that he was about to take in his theological thinking over the next few years. Throughout them, Newman's methodology is marked by the type of rationalism all pervasive in Anglican preaching since the time of John Tillotson in the seventeenth century. In its early days, Evangelicalism was hailed as a refreshing sea change to the cold, impersonal rationalism which Protestantism had inherited from the English Enlightenment. So pervasive was the rational approach in religion that Evangelicals were eventually obliged to adopt a similar approach when defending their own religious views. They thus presented a rational scheme of Christianity which had, as its central focus, Christ's atonement. Although extremely critical of individuals who highlighted one particular doctrine to the detriment of others and gave it 'an exclusive claim to the name of the Gospel',[6] Newman's own preaching up till 1828 was, in fact, an atonement-centred system. While the flavour of the contents was still often Evangelical, his method was decidedly rationalist.

Throughout these 1825 sermons, Newman presented revelation as a clear-cut system of haves versus have-nots, of light versus darkness. The world of light belonged to the Jewish and Christian dispensations, the only two, but by no means, co-equal partners in God's 'grand general scheme of revelation' beginning with Adam.[7] Beyond the world of light, lay a world of complete darkness inhabited by pagans who lived in perpetual ignorance of a supreme deity, and that included its best minds. Displays of compassion, love or humility were signs of human weakness.[8]

---

[5] Newman relied extensively on Wilson's lengthy introduction (161 pp.) to Butler's *Analogy of Religion, Natural and Revealed, to the Constitution and Course of Nature*, which he had just edited (Glasgow, 1824) and which Newman used to read Butler for the first time. He also relied on Erskine's *Remarks on the Internal Evidences for the Truth of Revealed Religion* (6th edn, Edinburgh, 1823).

[6] *U.S.* II, 34.

[7] Birmingham Oratory Archives (BOA) A 17.1, Sermon 110 (16 Oct. 1825), 'feelings produced in common to all revelations' (2), pp. 1–2.

[8] BO : A 17.1, Sermon 108 (5 Sept. 1825), 'on the principles common to all revelations', pp. 1–2.

According to Newman, now firmly under Whatelyan influence – but still clinging on to 'shreds and tatters' of Evangelicalism – two classes of revelation seemed to exist.[9] The first one was made up of doctrines which were the property of the Jewish and Christian dispensations, *equally* and *exclusively*. The second class of doctrines consisted of those which belonged to the Christian dispensation *exclusively*. Judaism and Christianity shared six doctrines in common: the 'existence of one and one only God'; the providence of that God who 'works in and by every thing, wisely, judiciously, and well'; a moral system controlled by rewards and punishments, administered by an 'Almighty Lawgiver'; an 'all-knowing, all-wise, good, merciful, true, just and holy' God; the fall of Adam and the subsequent corruption of the human race; and finally, God's promise of a Messiah.[10]

Provided people searched for these doctrines in the right frame of mind, they were discoverable by human reason and needed no direct divine intervention.[11] Because they did not do so, their best minds – yes, even the great Aristotle! – lived in blissful ignorance of the 'first principles of religion'. Perhaps one or two of them may have had a gut-feeling that a supreme deity existed somewhere or other. The bottom line was that the vast majority lived under the spell of, what Newman then referred to as an 'evil conscience'.[12] The result was, they were so 'cramped and shackled' by the burden of sin and corruption, they were blind to the 'seeds of truth' scattered in the 'waste wilderness', even with the 'book of nature' open and staring them in the face.[13]

Five further doctrines belonged exclusively to the Christian dispensation. Unlike the previous six, these were beyond reason, which is why we call them 'revealed' or 'evangelical' doctrines. They were communicated 'little by little' until 'all five became visible' and self-evident.[14] They focused on Jesus Christ. Of course, the jewel in the crown was Christ's atonement, the

[9] *Whatelyan*: reference to the influence of Richard Whately, Noetic and fellow of Oriel College from 1811–22; *Autobiographical Writings*, p. 78.

[10] Ibid., pp. 4–11; 16.

[11] V. F. Blehl, SJ (ed.), *John Henry Newman: Sermons 1824–1843*, p. 374; Sermon 119 (4 Dec. 1825), 'on natural religion'.

[12] Newman borrowed the term 'evil conscience' from a leading Evangelical, Charles Simeon (1759–1836). It was from Simeon that he gained his first understanding of the term 'conscience'. His reading of Butler's *Sermons* broadened his concept dramatically. It was a term he used in his earliest sermon on conscience (June 1825) which incorporates verbatim two of the five pages of a skeleton sermon by Simeon, entitled 'A Good and Evil Conscience'. See *Helps to Composition: or, Six Hundred Skeletons of Sermons*, Vol. IV, 299–303 (3rd edn, London, 1815).

[13] Ibid., p. 379; Sermon 108, p. 18.

[14] Ibid., pp. 373–4.

'only warrantable foundation' on which eternal life was possible. There was 'no good reason' for supposing that it was appreciated in its full glory by the Jews. Nor were they given a clue to the Messiah's identity. God deliberately delayed implementation of the full divine plan until at least some of the people of Israel realised how totally and incurably corrupt the human race really was. Had God revealed the divine plan for a saving expiatory sacrifice before such a conviction had been arrived at, its impact would have been anti-climactic. And so Christ's atonement has ever since appealed so profoundly, yet so reasonably, to the human race.[15] The other four exclusive doctrines were: eternal punishment; pardon on repentance; sanctifying grace for the individual; and finally, the promise of eternal happiness.

While many aspects of the gospel message were beyond reason, there was much also that was 'agreeable' to it. Revealed truth demonstrated that the God of nature and the God of Scripture were one and the same deity. Admittedly, no one could possibly deduce from nature that the long-awaited Messiah was to be God's only son. Once it occurred, however, the whole scheme dovetailed neatly and reasonably into the natural scheme of things where the rich mediated for the poor, the learned for the ignorant, the strong for the weak, the old for the young, the innocent for the guilty, the just for the unjust. If mediation was a great mystery in nature, then Christ's atonement was an even greater mystery in supernature.[16]

Protestant refusal to allow for any measure of divine light penetrating into the darkness of the heathen world relied for its mainstay on the thirteenth article of the Thirty-nine Articles. Entitled 'Of Works before Justification', Article XIII declared that any works, 'done before the grace of Christ, and the Inspiration of his Spirit, are not pleasant to God, forasmuch as they spring not of faith in Jesus Christ, neither do they make men meet to receive grace, or (as the School-authors say) deserve grace of congruity: yea rather, for that they are not done as God willed and commanded them to be done, we doubt not but they have the nature of sin'. Article XIII was frequently used by both ultra-Protestants and liberals in their rather different attempts to create apologetic bulwarks against Unitarians on one side, and Roman Catholics on the other. So strong, indeed, was its authority, that Newman himself continued to stress its importance from the university pulpit, three years after beginning to shake off the influence of Whately, and some time after his first encounter with

[15] Ibid., pp. 354f.; Sermon 112 (30 Oct. 1825), 'on the knowledge of the gospel in the *antediluvian* age'.
[16] Ibid., pp. 381f.; Sermon 123 (11 Dec. 1825), 'on the internal evidence of the evangelical doctrine'.

the Alexandrian Fathers who were so seminal in broadening his horizons in this area.[17]

Even before resigning his curacy at St Clement's and accepting a tutorship at Oriel, the Evangelical traces in his thinking had grown fainter, though the Whatelyan influence continued undiluted.[18] It has been suggested that, when he confessed in the *Apologia* to 'drifting in the direction of the Liberalism of the day', Newman was exaggerating and doing nothing of the sort.[19] The truth is that he did dally with it for a time, as sermons of the period clearly indicate.[20] For example, in one particular sermon, he maintained that Christian liberty 'consists in our knowing in great measure the *reasons* of the divine commands and having strong motives for complying with them . . . in opposition to a blind obedience'; and that the Gospels contained '*principles* which act as *foundations* for a large and enlightened *knowledge* of our duty, as *sanctions* for *enforcing* it upon us, and as *motives* for our *performing* it'.[21] In yet another sermon of this period, he argued that the Trinity is not 'one doctrine, but a *set of doctrines*, collected together and viewed in a particular light by the Church'; that it is a set of 'scriptural facts reduced to order by man'; that 'our rational belief in it becomes a test of our having examined it carefully and humbly';

---

[17] See *U.S.* III, 41, 'Evangelical Sanctity the Completion of Natural Virtue', preached 6 March 1831. In *Tract* 90, Newman offered some important, and controversial, considerations concerning Article XIII: 'The Article contemplates these two states, – one of justifying grace, and one of the utter destitution of grace; and it says, that those who are in utter destitution cannot do anything to gain justification; and, indeed, to assert the contrary would be Pelagianism. However, there is an intermediate state, of which the Article says nothing, but which must not be forgotten as being an actual existing one. Men are not always in light or darkness, but are sometimes between the two; they are sometimes not in a state of Christian justification, yet not utterly deserted by God, but in a state something like that of Jews or of Heathen, turning to the thought of religion. They are not gifted with *habitual* grace, but they are still visited by Divine influences, or by *actual* grace, or rather *aid*; and these influences are the first fruits of the grace of justification going before it, and are intended to lead on to it, and be perfected in it, as twilight leads to day . . . such were Cornelius's alms, fastings, and prayers, which led to his baptism' (*V.M.* II, 286).

[18] Indeed, we find Newman retrospectively tagging certain sermons of this period 'Whatelyan'.

[19] *Apologia pro Vita Sua (Apo.)*, pp. 13–4. See A. J. Boekraad, *The Personal Conquest of Truth*, p. 97.

[20] Among authors Newman was consulting throughout this period was the Dutch Arminian, Hugo Grotius (1583–1645). At the same time, his friend, Edward Bouverie Pusey, who was studying with Ernst Rosenmüller (1768–1835) in Göttingen and Friedrich Schleiermacher (1768–1834) in Berlin, was warning Newman against the rationalising implications of making distinctions between apostolic and post-apostolic miracles.

[21] BO : A 50.1, 2 September 1827, 'On the Christian law of liberty', pp. 4, 4a, 13–14.

31

and that 'it seems intended to teach us that our belief in it must be *practical*, not merely intellectual and abstract'.[22]

Towards the end of 1827, he was rudely woken from this flirtation with Anglican liberalism by a breakdown in his own health and by the unexpected death of his favourite and youngest sister, Mary.[23] Both events coincided with his initial reading of Justin Martyr, together with his second reading of Joseph Butler – this time, in the spirit of a John Keble instead of a Richard Whately or a Renn Dickson Hampden. The result was that he began sloughing off his earlier narrow ideas on revelation and began warming to the idea of universal revelation. It was Justin Martyr who first introduced him to the *possibility*; and Butler's teaching on personal conscience which provided the *means* by which God had revealed certain divine truths to the whole human race, independently of Judaism and Christianity.

Newman first studied Butler's *Analogy of Religion* in July 1825, less than a month after ordination to the priesthood and three months after his appointment by Whately as vice-Principal to St Alban. Turning to this classic text would have been natural for a young fellow of Oriel, whose Noetic members held Butler in such high regard. It has recently been pointed out that, in the works of liberal Oriel divines, direct references to Butler's writing were just as common as quotes from John Locke. Butler's comments on the 'uncertainty of human knowledge, on the difficulty of fully understanding the revealed message, as well as the natural and moral worlds, were understandably appealing to the apologetic aims of Copleston, Whately and Baden Powell'.[24] Renn Dickson Hampden himself boasted that he had 'endeavoured to exemplify' the 'spirit' of Butler's *Analogy* in all that he had written', and, furthermore, that he had been 'mainly instrumental in introducing the works of Butler into the course of reading for Academical Honours' at Oxford in 1833.[25]

Butler used the analogy between natural and revealed religion to point out that the inconsistencies and absurdities ascribed by Deists to the

---

[22] BO : A 50.1, 1 June 1828, 'On the doctrine of the Trinity', pp. 5, 21.

[23] In November 1827, Newman suffered a breakdown similar to the one that prevented him from gaining first-class honours in 1820. Mary died on 5 January 1828, possibly of a heart attack.

[24] P. Corsi, *Science and Religion: Baden Powell and the Anglican debate, 1800–1860* (Cambridge: Cambridge University Press, 1988), pp. 76–7. Corsi goes on to challenge rightly the argument of W. Fey that 'Newman "found in Butler a fresh alternative to the artificial reasoning of the Noetics" by arguing that the 'view that the Noetics were anti-Butlerians is not new'.

[25] R. Brent, *Liberal Anglican Politics: Whiggery, Religion, and Reform: 1830–1841* (Oxford: Clarendon Press, 1987), pp. 153–4.

contents of Christian revelation were matched equally by the same sort of problems, or at least the same sort of perplexities, in the type of natural religion favoured by the likes of Tindall, Chubb and Toland. One of the problems with this approach was that it could be used to argue that agnosticism, even atheism, was an equally rational alternative to Christianity. Even well into the nineteenth century, the Butlerian blueprint was worked and reworked time and again, not least by Oxford scholars.

The Butlerian resort to analogy also guided the Oriel men in their choice of answer to a dilemma created by their firm adherence to Locke's empiricism which maintained that true knowledge can only come from experience. While Locke constructed his empiricism in such a way as to make the existence of God one of the most immediate and obvious fruits of experiential knowledge, it still did not resolve the status of certain theological categories and terms. In talking of a God who was 'all-wise' or 'all-knowing', theologians were merely ascribing human qualities to the deity, thereby fatally compromising God's divinity. The answer to this problem was that we can only claim to have knowledge of God that was analogous rather than direct. We make no claim to know anything about God as God really *is*, only as God is *relative* to us. According to people like Whately and Hampden, 'knowledge from experience was of facts relative to the observer' and nothing more.[26] The purpose of Christ's coming was to teach of religion connected with moral matters. Doctrinal matters were only relevant in so far as they were 'practical' in assisting fulfilling one's duties.

In recounting his debt to Butler, Newman identified two points of outstanding value – the doctrine of analogy and the importance of probability in bringing individuals to personal belief. 'Butler's doctrine that Probability is the guide of life, led me, at least under the teaching to which a few years later I was introduced, to the question of the logical cogency of Faith.'[27] The 'few years later' should be noted carefully. In the mid-1820s, Newman's thinking was still a very long way from his later understanding of 'how we could be *certain* on probabilities'.[28] For Noetics, a rather loose 'practical certainty' was provided by Butler's argument from probability, and for them, that was good enough. On these points at this stage, Newman would have been satisfied to follow his mentor Whately who was quite dismissive of anyone who displayed an 'aversion to doubt'. For him, 'practical certainty' could not eliminate doubt, and nor should it. He insisted that 'he who would cultivate an habitual devotion to Truth,

---

[26] R. Brent, op. cit., p. 158.
[27] Apo., pp. 10–11.
[28] *Letters and Diaries of John Henry Newman*, (L.D.), XXI, 129.

must be solicitous in the first place to avoid error, and must consequently in all cases prefer *doubt* to the reception of falsehood'.[29]

In 1827, Newman was brought back to Butler's key themes, but this time via a different agency – John Keble and his *Christian Year* which had just been published. In Keble's teaching, Butler's doctrine of analogy becomes the key for understanding the 'Sacramental system' which was the 'doctrine that material phenomena are both the types and the instruments of real things unseen, – a doctrine, which embraces in its fulness, . . . Sacraments properly so called', and 'also the article of "the Communion of Saints"', as well as the 'Mysteries of the faith'.[30] While Keble did not seek to use Butler's doctrine of analogy to attain a theory of anything greater than 'practical certainty', he stressed the living power of faith, and the living power of love for the object of that faith', already existing in the mind that accepted the probabilities. Such teaching helped to lift Newman's understanding above the arid rationalism of the Noetics, though it was still a far cry from the undoubting assent which was to be the focus of his greatest work of apologetics, *The Grammar of Assent*.[31] Now, there was also a third Butlerian theme which entered Newman's horizon at this time – personal conscience. And it was this component which was to change his understanding of the religious position of sincere heathens.

For Butler, personal conscience is not just another human faculty among many. By its very nature, it is 'anterior to the Gospel', bearing the seal of its own authority.[32] To treat it like any other faculty was a 'violation' of human nature. From the very nature of the individual, conscience, and conscience alone, had the right to dictate human behaviour. 'Had it strength, as it has right; had it power, as it has manifest authority, it would absolutely govern the world.'[33] Not only did conscience point people in the right direction, it was a 'natural guide' which must be obeyed at all times and in all situations. That was God's plan.[34]

The second breakthrough came when Newman started reading Justin Martyr round about the same time. In retrospect, he overlooked the fact that it was Justin who first introduced him to the idea of revelation outside

<hr>

[29] R. Whately, *Essays (second series) on Some of the Difficulties of the Writings of the Apostle Paul* . . . (4th edn, London, 1837), p. 35. It is ironic to reflect that, fifteen or so years later, Newman was emphatic that faith and doubt were mutually exclusive.

[30] *Apo.*, p. 18.

[31] Newman later reflected sadly that, in Keble's view, 'faith was not a clear and confident knowledge or certainty, but a sort of loving guess' (*L.D.*), XXI, 129.

[32] Sermon I, 2; Sermon II, 11.

[33] Sermon II, 18–19.

[34] Sermon III, 6.

the Jewish and Christian dispensations, not Clement of Alexandria and Origen as he originally indicated in the *Apologia* where he tells us that the 'broad philosophy of Clement and Origen' carried him away as a young man.[35] The fact of the matter is that it was not Clement, and definitely not Origen whose general attitude to Greek philosophy was critical and uncompromising.[36] Clement was instrumental in broadening his horizons on the matter, but that was around three years after Justin had introduced him to the idea of the *Logos spermatikos* in 1828. Collectively, they fired Newman's imagination on the subject:

> Some portions of their teaching, magnificent in themselves, came like music to my inward ear, as if the response to ideas, which, with little external to encourage them, I had cherished so long. They were based on the mystical or sacramental principle, and spoke of various Economies or Dispensations of the Eternal. I understood these passages to mean that the exterior world, physical and historical, was but the outward manifestation to our senses of realities greater than itself. Nature was a parable: Scripture was an allegory: pagan literature, philosophy, and mythology, properly understood, were but a preparation for the Gospel. The Greek poets and sages were in a certain sense prophets; for 'thoughts beyond their thought to those high bards were given'. There had been a directly divine dispensation granted to the Jews; but there had been in some sense a dispensation carried on in favour of the Gentiles. He who had taken the seed of Jacob for His elect people had not therefore cast the rest of mankind out of His sight.[37]

In the Johannine tradition, Justin Martyr believed that the divine *Logos* (Jesus Christ) had sown seeds of divine truth in every age, race and individual. These he called the *Logos spermatikos*, God's purpose being to give everyone everywhere access to eternal truths, however fragmentary and obscure. In a special way, God had singled out the Greeks to implant in their hearts and minds seeds of divine truth so that they could, in a special way, 'participate in the life of the *Logos*'.[38] It was never Justin's intention to draw a detailed map of the relationship between Hellenism and Christianity. His was a personal expression of faith in the pre-existent Christ, who had been quietly at work among the Greeks for hundreds of years. He wanted to give an honourable place to pagan literature in the Christian scheme of things and to establish the status of a Homer or a Plato within that system. He stopped short of saying that such seeds were

[35] *Apo.*, p. 26.
[36] See H. Chadwick (tr.), *Origen: Contra Celsum* (Cambridge: Cambridge University Press, 1953), Book VI, Sect. 3–4, pp. 317–18.
[37] *Apo.*, pp. 26–7.
[38] Justin Martyr, 2 *Apology* 13:83; 10:79–80.

an actual preparation for the Gospel. Clement of Alexandria thought they were and said so.

Newman's writings of the period reflect the new direction his thinking was now taking. Back in 1825, he had accused Aristotle of being 'grossly ignorant' of his moral duty to God and his neighbour.[39] But now, five years later, he begins to see certain similarities between him and the patriarch Abraham. He now sees that when Aristotle made such statements as: 'I will follow moral excellence without reference to the pleasure which may or may not attend it, because it is good and my best instincts prompt me to follow it', he is doing what Abraham had done, taking 'God as his portion without definite promise'. By trusting the 'voice of God' without thought of the consequences, both individuals were displaying the 'same self neglect and self denial, and resolute and noble disinterestedness'.[40] In a sermon of the same period, he now states that 'many an ungifted heathen' like Rahab, Naaman and Cornelius, with their single talent, probably lived 'better and holier lives' than many Christians. On the day of general judgement, they may well put the rest of us to shame.[41]

Again, in the following February, Newman preached a sermon, employing language and imagery similar to later statements which would occur in *Arians of the Fourth Century* (1834), *Lectures on Justification* (1838) and *Essay on Development* (1845):

> Our blessed Saviour came to build up and put in order the house of God which men's sins since the fall have broken to pieces. He was not content to reveal religious truths and let them take their chance course – to send down His gift of grace to dwell unknown in the world, as in former ages, – He lodged His gifts in a home where men might go for them and be sure to find – He collected together the remnants of those former revelations by which men know their duty and put them into form; he confirmed them and added to them . . . Before He came truth had been for the most part in pilgrimage – and the voice of God had been uncertain, and irregularly heard.[42]

Arians of the Fourth Century provided him with an ideal opportunity for an extended treatment on the subject, now that he had absorbed Clement of Alexandria's comments about Hellenism and Christianity sharing a common tradition and Greek culture being a preparation for the Gospels.[43]

---

[39] BO Sermon 106, p. 5.

[40] BO : A 7.1.

[41] BO, Sermon 198, p. 6., 'The Christian's spiritual obedience; – the holy Spirit the author of it', preached 7 June 1829.

[42] BO Sermon 228, pp. 8–9, 'The Liturgy, *first*, teaches doctrine, – viz. concerning means of grace', 28 February 1830.

[43] *Arians of the Fourth Century* (Ari.), Ch. I, Sect. III, part 5, 'The Dispensation of Paganism', pp. 79–89.

According to Newman, the word *dispensation* had several meanings. Paul the Apostle used it in his epistle to the Ephesians to describe a series of divine 'appointments viewed as whole, by which the Gospel is introduced and realized' among the human race. In a wider sense, it encompasses the Jewish, patriarchal and any other divine process 'greater or less', which consists of means and an end. In an even wider sense, it can also apply to the 'general system' of divine providence 'by which the world's course is carried on'. It can even apply to creation itself. In whatever sense it is used, all such dispensations reveal God's character in action and are simply allowances for the limitations of the human mind. They are 'shadowy representations of realities' about which we know virtually nothing.[44]

In examining the Church of Alexandria's attitude to paganism in *Arians*, Newman poses the question: 'In what sense can it be said, that there is any connection between Paganism and Christianity so real, as to warrant the preacher of the latter to conciliate idolaters by allusion to it?' In making connections between Paganism and Christianity, the Alexandrian Church used Paul the Apostle as 'sufficient guide' and 'full justification' for doing so.

Revealed religion contains doctrines taught in the Jewish and Christian dispensations. They originate from God in a way 'in which no other doctrine' does. Yet, on the authority of Scripture itself, we are informed that 'all knowledge of religion' is of divine origin and not just that special knowledge transmitted via the Old and New Testament. In fact, declares Newman, there has never been a time when God has not spoken to the human race and instructed it in its duties. 'It would seem, then, that there is something true and divinely revealed, in every religion all over the earth.' This includes belief in the 'power and presence of an invisible God', God's moral law and governance, our duty at all times to do the right thing, and the inevitability of a just judgement with rewards and punishments to follow. Revelation is a 'universal', not a local gift. The difference between Judaism and Christianity on the one hand, and paganism on the other, is not the difference between who goes to heaven or who goes to hell. The difference is that the 'elect people of God' have always had, and the rest of humanity never did have, Scripture and the sacraments as divinely appointed channels of communication. Nevertheless, every individual has always had 'more or less the guidance of Tradition, in addition to those internal notions of right and wrong' deposited in his or her conscience:

> This vague and uncertain family of religious truths, originally from God, but sojourning without the sanction of miracle, or a definite home, as pilgrims up

[44] Ibid., pp. 74–5.

and down the world, and discernible and separable from the corrupt legends with which they are mixed, by the spiritual mind alone, may be called the *Dispensation of Paganism*.[45]

As well as including a patriarchal record, the book of Genesis also contains a record of such a dispensation. The dreams of Pharaoh, Abimelech and Nebuchadnezzar are obvious examples of God's relationship with individuals outside Judaism. Job himself was an outsider who was rewarded for his faithfulness when he heard the 'voice of God out of the whirlwind'. Again, the story of Balaam, another outsider, who, in spite of his dubious reputation, became God's messenger about 'doing justly, and loving mercy, and walking humbly'. Even on the 'altars of superstition' the Holy Spirit utters prophesies. If we accept this, then there is nothing startling in the idea that there may have been heathen poets and sages who were divinely inspired and who conveyed 'religious and moral' truths to 'their countrymen'.[46]

At different times in his later years at Oxford, Newman clashed with several liberal thinkers of the day who thought that, while there was much 'truth and value' in primitive Christianity, it also contained doctrines contrary to reason. To differentiate between reasonable and unreasonable doctrines in God's revelation, they applied the principle that, if any so-called doctrine betrayed traces of 'Platonism, or Judaism, or Paganism', then it was not part of Christian revelation. For example, the mystical efficacy of the sacraments had its roots in Platonism, church order in Judaism, and ritualism in paganism. Since this was obviously the case, as indeed it was, they concluded that these were *not* authentic revelation. Newman both agreed and disagreed with this line of argument. He preferred an alternative principle: namely, since 'much of authentic Christian revelation can generally be found in other religions, philosophies and cultures, either in part or in whole', they must be recognised and accepted as authentic revelation:

> In the sense in which the doctrine of the Trinity is Platonic, doubtless the doctrine of mysteries generally is Platonic also. . . . Unbelievers have accused Moses of borrowing his law from the Egyptians or other Pagans . . . though even if proved, and so far as proved, it would show nothing more than this, – that God, who gave His law to Israel absolutely and openly, had already given some portions of it to the heathen.[47]

[45] Ibid., pp. 79–81. In addition to calling it a Dispensation of Paganism, Newman also used other terms: 'the Divinity of Paganism'; 'the divinity of Traditionary Religion'; and 'the Dispensation of Natural Religion', pp. 75, 81, 83.

[46] Ibid., pp. 81–2.

[47] *Discussions and Arguments on Various Subjects*, pp. 202–3, 210–11.

If the doctrine of the Trinity is of Platonic origins, so too is the 'ceremony of washing', the 'rite of sacrifice' and the 'doctrine of the Divine Word'. Furthermore:

> . . . the doctrine of the Incarnation is Indian; of a divine kingdom is Judaic; of Angels and demons is Magian; the connexion of sin with the body is Gnostic; celibacy is known to Bonze and Talapoin; a sacerdotal order is Egyptian; the idea of a new birth is Chinese and Eleusinian; belief in sacramental virtue is Pythagorean; and honours to the dead are a polytheism.[48]

In his *Essay on the Development of Christian Doctrine*, Newman examines Christianity's particular gift for absorbing ideas from other religious systems, without sacrificing any inherent goodness. All religious systems possess the 'same great and comprehensive subject-matter'. From its very beginning, Christianity was surrounded on all sides by 'rites, sects, and philosophies, which contemplated the same questions, advocated the same truths', and bore 'the same external appearance'. The big difference was that Christianity acknowledged 'all truth and revelation' as originating from one supreme deity who had never left the human race without a witness, and now, in the person of Jesus Christ, that God had come 'not to undo the past, but to fulfil and perfect it'. In spite of two thousand years of 'collision and conflict', Christianity succeeded in 'purifying, assimilating, transmuting, and taking into itself the many-coloured beliefs, forms of worship, codes of duty, schools of thought, through which it was ever moving':[49]

> True religion is the summit and perfection of false religions; it combines in one whatever there is of good and true separately remaining in each. And in like manner the Catholic Creed is for the most part the combination of separate truths. . . . So that, in matter of fact, if a religious mind were educated in and sincerely attached to some form of heathenism or heresy, and then were brought under the light of truth, it would be drawn off from error into the truth, not by losing what it had, but by gaining what it had not, not by being unclothed, but by being 'clothed upon'. . . . True conversion is ever of a positive, not a negative character.[50]

---

[48] *Essays Critical and Historical* II, 230–1. *Bonze*: Buddhist monks from Japan and China; *Talapoin*: Buddhist monks from Burma and Cambodia; *Eleusinian* refers to the town of Eleusis, north-west of Athens, where the Eleusinian mysteries of Demeter were celebrated. Demeter was goddess of corn and mother of Persephone who was abducted by Hades and brought to his kingdom of the dead. A distraught Demeter inflicted such a disastrous drought on the land that Zeus had to intervene. It was finally agreed that Persephone would spend spring and summer with Demeter, and winter and autumn in the kingdom of the dead. In the Eleusinian mysteries, we encounter a theme common in the ancient world, namely, that, in dying and rising again to life, new growth becomes a symbol of spiritual regeneration.

[49] *An Essay on the Development of Christian Doctrine*, pp. 355–7.

[50] Ibid., pp. 200–1.

It is, suggests Newman, the 'very nature' of 'true philosophy' to be 'polemical, eclectic' and 'unitive'. By trusting in the continuity and strength of her principles, Christianity successfully assimilated customs and practices which another religious system would have found 'incompatible' with its own belief system. The Church has never hesitated or scrupled in absorbing Gnostic and Platonic ideas as, for example, when it acknowledged the link between Platonism and the Incarnation in the opening chapter of John's Gospel. She confidently takes on board whatever 'appendages and instruments' she needs from local rites and practices, knowing that, if she did not utilise them, she would have to invent what she needed, knowing that she was already in possession of the original archetypes. For example:

> The use of temples, and these dedicated to particular saints, and ornamented on occasions with branches of trees; incense, lamps, and candles; votive offerings on recovery from illness; holy water; asylums; holydays and seasons, use of calendars, processions, blessings on the fields; sacerdotal vestments, the tonsure, the ring in marriage, turning to the East, images at a later date, perhaps the ecclesiastical chant, and the Kyrie Eleison, are all of pagan origin, and sanctified by their adoption into the Church.[51]

Newman's love for the classics never faltered. Xenophon remained one of the 'best principled and most religious' writers who ever lived;[52] Virgil a prophet whose very 'half sentences' were 'thrilling oracles' which spoke directly to the human heart. No one was ever so solemn, so 'severe in taste' and so 'austerely beautiful' as Sophocles; and nobody as faithful to the 'great laws of divine governance, providence and immutability'.[53] He applauded Athenian life in the age of Pericles for its democratic principles. To the great credit of its citizens, its great orators had formulated a 'beautiful idea' which, though not fully realised in those golden years, was a precursor of the Kingdom of Christ.[54]

He was also convinced that Greek ethics was too much like Christian ethics to be coincidence.[55] On personal conscience, Cicero, Aeschylus, Origen and Tertullian were 'always consistent with one another'. They agreed that conscience commands, praises, blames, threatens, and holds

[51] Ibid., pp. 371–3.
[52] *Sermons preached on Various Occasions* (O.S.), p. 23.
[53] *Letters and Diaries of John Henry Newman*, (L.D.), XX, 548. In the fourth poem of his *Eclogues*, Virgil reflects on the common belief of his day that a messiah was about to appear and rescue the world from the mess it found itself in.
[54] *Historical Sketches* III (H.S.), III, 86.
[55] H. M. de Achaval, SJ, and J. D. Holmes (eds.), *The Theological Papers of John Henry Newman on Faith and Certainty* (Oxford: Clarendon Press, 1976), p. 138.

out the promise of a life beyond the here and now. It is more than a person's 'own self'. Try as we can, we cannot control it. We 'did not make it', we 'cannot destroy it'. We 'can silence it' for a time, we can distort it, but we cannot run away from it forever. It will stalk us till the day we die, no matter where we go and what we do.[56]

One of the first Christians who recognised that the idea of a Dispensation of Paganism was in harmony with Christ's teaching was Paul the Apostle.[57] Together with Athanasius and John Chrysostom, Paul belonged to that special breed for whom divine grace invigorated, elevated and ennobled human nature.[58] Even after his conversion, Paul continued to live as an ordinary human being, human nature losing none of its vigour. The result was 'that, having the nature of man so strong within him, he was able to enter into human nature, and so sympathise with it, with a gift peculiarly his own'. Divine grace had left him in full control of his humanity. He knew the world so intimately and understood the human heart so profoundly that God had entrusted him with the mission of evangelising the Gentiles. Compassion was his method of conversion and love the fountainhead of his authority. His 'remarkable' admiration for Greek literature contributed to his success as an evangeliser. Just as Moses was acquainted with the wisdom of Egypt, so Paul was acquainted with the wisdom of Greece. He loved 'poor human nature', and the 'literature of the Greeks was only its expression'. He contemplated it 'tenderly and mournfully, wishing for regeneration and salvation', because, like Justin and Clement after him, he was convinced 'that the Greeks were under a special dispensation of Providence, preparatory to the Gospel'.[59]

When Newman was an eighty-two years old and a cardinal, W. S. Lilly, secretary to the Catholic Union of England, sent him an article entitled 'The Sacred Books of the East' which he had written especially for the *Dublin Review*.[60] In it, Lilly singled out for special mention Newman's 'weighty words' on a Dispensation of Paganism in *Arians of the Fourth Century*.[61] In reply, a delighted Newman thanked him for his generosity. Since *Arians* had been his first published book almost fifty years ago, he had become aware of its inexactness in 'thought' and incorrectness in 'language' and that it needed a thorough overhaul, but that was something

[56] E. J. Sillem (ed.), *John H. Newman, The Philosophical Notebook* II (Louvain: Nauwelaerts Publishing House, 1970), pp. 53–6.
[57] H.S. III, 60.
[58] O.S., pp. 92–3.
[59] Ibid., pp. 95–8, 114, 103.
[60] 'The Sacred Books of the East', *Dublin Review* (July, 1882), pp. 28–32. Lilly later included it as Chapter 3 in *Ancient Religion and Modern Thought* (London, 1884).
[61] *Ari.*, pp. 81–6.

he was not going to undertake, not at this stage of his life. Whatever its faults and failings, however, he had 'no intention of withdrawing from the substance' of what he had written about a Dispensation of Paganism. On the contrary, 'I hold it as strongly as I did fifty years ago when it was written'.[62]

---

[62] *L.D.*, XXX, 105.

Newman's Application of the Offices of the Church in the Search for a Reformed Catholicism

HALBERT WEIDNER

J OHN HENRY NEWMAN's theology of the triple offices of the Church became a foundation for a theology on abuses in the Church. This theology was central to his life-long search for a reformed Catholicism. It is well worth more study during the present cultural crisis that engulfs a good portion of today's Christian Church as well as the worlds of education, government, and economics.[1] The purpose of this article will be to review some major points of Newman's thought on why a Church that is, according to the Creed, 'one, holy, catholic, and apostolic,' is so perpetually in need of reform.[2] The conclusion of the article will consider a few applications of Newman to pastoral theology today. The writer is an active Roman Catholic pastor who has some idea that parochial exigencies

---

[1] That there is such a crisis seems evident from a variety of authors who seem to be doing more than indulging in rhetorical 'viewing with alarm': Robert Conquest, *Reflections on a Ravaged Century* (New York: W. W. Norton & Co., 2000), Alain Finkielkraut, *The Defeat of the Mind* (New York: Columbia University Press, 1995), Susan Haack, *Manifesto of a Passionate Moderate* (University of Chicago Press, 1998), Jacques Barzun, *From Dawn to Decadence* (New York: Harper Collins, 2000), Noretta Koertge (ed.), *A House Built on Sand* (New York: Oxford University Press, 1998). Perhaps the wider cultural question might be whether or not we can ever reform all the things in our society that need it.

[2] The classic fuller treatment of the question is found in John Henry Newman's preface to the third edition of *The Via Media of the Anglican Church* (Oxford: Clarendon Press, 1990), pp. 10–57. The term 'theology of abuses in the Church' comes from Maurice Nédoncelle, 'Newman, théologien des abus de l'Eglise,' *Oecumenica*, ii (1967), pp. 116–32.

can corrupt the theological enterprise while at the same time theological categories can simplify and falsify the map of daily life where the Church lives. Since most of Newman's theology emerged from such pastoral questions and not from a deliberate system, it seems appropriate to sketch such suggestions as a Kindly Light may later allow as steps away from the encircling gloom.

The first point of light would be to begin with a description of catholicity in its ideal form found in Avery Dulles' *The Catholicity of the Church:*

> The concept of catholicity, being analogous rather than univocal, does not admit of any precise definition, but it can be distinguished from other similar concepts such as fullness and universality. Unlike universality, catholicity is a concrete term: it is predicated not of abstract essences but of particular, existing realities. Furthermore, it always implies intensity, richness, and plenitude. Unlike fullness, it implies a unitive relationship among things that are diverse ... Catholicity, far from excluding differences, demands them. In all the instances of catholicity we have considered – Trinity, Incarnation, Church, and world – we have found a union of opposites that might, in themselves, seem incompatible. Finally, catholicity is a dynamic term. It designates a fullness of reality and life, especially divine life, actively communicating itself. This life, flowing outwards, pulsates through many subjects, draws them together, and brings them into union with their source and goal.[3]

One of the chief purposes of reform and renewal in the Church is to make more effective the power of its catholicity. Today one of the liveliest questions in ecumenical theology and in pastoral practice concerns the extent of renewal needed for the sake of catholicity. This question was of paramount interest to Newman. We will investigate the question from an experience of the Roman Catholic Church. We can do this because it was Newman's own concrete situation and because Roman Catholicism exhibits most of catholicity's virtues and nearly all of its problems. The condition of the Roman Catholic Church in Newman's time could hardly have been less critical than today's situation. Newman wrote in the 1877 preface to the *Via Media*: 'It is so ordered from on high that in our day Holy Church should present just that aspect to my countrymen which is most consonant with their ingrained prejudices against her, most unpromising for their conversion; and what can one writer do to counteract this misfortune?'[4] In private correspondence much earlier, Newman had been as blunt. In a letter of 1863 to fiction writer Lady Henrietta Chatterton, he had said, 'Doubtless the face of the Visible Church is very disappointing to an earnest

---

[3] Avery Dulles, SJ, *The Catholicity of the Church* (Oxford: Clarendon Press), p. 167.

[4] John Henry Newman, *The Via Media of the Anglican Church*, H. D. Weidner (ed.) (Oxford: Clarendon Press, 1990), p. 23.

mind, nay, in a certain sense, a scandal. I assert, rather than grant, this grave and remarkable fact'.[5] Newman would draw on the outline of this letter for his theology of abuses in the Church sketched in the Roman Catholic preface to a third edition of his Anglican work on the Prophetical Office: *The Via Media of the Anglican Church*, I.

Newman's specific contribution in the Preface was to draw attention to the traditional three offices of Christ as they applied to the Church's ministry: teaching, sanctifying, and governing. His originality lay in seeing that these three offices were given to the Church in a human measure and therefore their totally fair coordination would be impossible. Even as a Roman Catholic, the belief in the infallibility of the teaching office did not, could not, guarantee impeccable exercise of the governing and sanctifying offices. Churches that do not accept an infallible teaching office experience even a more human exercise of the offices of Christ. What resources did Newman use for developing this theology and what practical use is it today?

In Newman, we can begin with the thirteenth chapter of the Gospel of Matthew. This chapter is the central discourse on the mystery of the reign of God. With the parables here, Jesus upsets the purity and strength of the kingdom of God popularly expected. Instead, Jesus says it will be a field of weeds and wheat, a dragnet with trash and fish until the angels come and sort it out. For Newman, this was an explicitly ecclesial text. He had said to Lady Chatterton: '. . . our Lord distinctly predicted these scandals as inevitable; nay further, He spoke of His Church in its very constitution made up of good and bad, of wheat and weeds, of the precious and the vile'.[6] Here we find the word church used and even the foundations for an argument on a Petrine ministry within the Church. At the same time Matthew's Jesus speaks of church and changes Simon's name to Peter or 'Rock,' the same Jesus rebukes the same Peter for standing in the way of the cross necessary for the messiah. It is within the discourses of Jesus in this ecclesial Gospel that Newman found the basis for a theology of church abuses and the basis for the need of an ever-renewing catholic Christianity. It is in the central discourse of Matthew 13 that we find the parable of the kingdom of heaven being a field where wheat and weeds grow together so closely that to tear out the weeds endangers the wheat. We also find the parable of the kingdom of heaven being like a net that drags fish and debris up out of the water. The net will always do this until the angels come on

[5] John Henry Newman, *Letters and Diaries*, XX, Charles Stephen Dessain (ed.) (London: Nelson, 1970), p. 465.

[6] *Letters and Diaries*, XX, p. 465. A few years later, Lady Chatterton and her husband were received by Newman into full communion with the Roman Catholic Church.

the last day. The waters never yield anything like a simple catch of fish. These parables clearly mark out the dilemma of the Church from its foundations. It should not be news that the Church is constrained by sinful members. But in the media sin sells and the sins of the Church sell the best. So the counter witness of Christians is news even if this is an old story. And so what Newman says in 1877 in the face of Victorian tabloids applies today: 'it will always be easy for her [the Church's] enemies to make a case against her, well founded or not, from the action or interaction, or the chronic collisions or contrasts, or the temporary suspense or delay, of her administration, in these three several departments of duty – her government, her devotions, and her schools – from the conduct of her rules, her divines, her pastors, or her people'.[7]

Newman's concerns, though, went beyond the obviousness of unworthy Christians to something deeper: the inability of the Church as Church to function in a completely faithful way even though it is one, holy, catholic and apostolic. Further it is the very fact that a Church sharing in the triple offices of Christ as priest, king, and prophet suffers inadequacies beyond the sinfulness of individual members.

The linkage of the Creedal formula of the four marks of the Church with the triple offices of Christ shared in by the Church, Newman found among other places in Bishop John Pearson's seventeenth-century *Exposition of the Creed*. Pearson is acknowledged as an outstanding scholar and theologian in the Church of England at a time of many great scholars and theologians. He was an early and primary introduction for Newman to both the Caroline Anglican theologians as well as patristics.[8] Pearson is defending the Church of England as the Church of the Nicene Creed as well as teaching that this body shares as church in the three offices of Christ. His teaching, shared later by Newman and many others, used patristic sources for an ecclesiology drawn from the four notes of the Church in the Creed with Calvinist sources that united the three offices of Christ – king, prophet, and priest. The temptation in such an ecclesiology is to divinize the Church. Indeed, against Puritan assaults on the Episcopacy, it was meant to be a very strong defense of a Church identified both with the Creed and with the triple ministries of Christ.

The uniqueness of Newman is his strong defense of the Church using the same theology as Pearson yet at the same time exploring why this strong ecclesiology also explains the weaknesses of the Church in its

---

[7] *Via Media*, p. 27.

[8] This encounter with Pearson dates at least from 1828. See John Henry Newman, *Letters and Diaries*, II, Ian Ker and Thomas Gornall, SJ (ed.) (Oxford: Clarendon Press, 1979), p. 81, as well as my introduction to Newman's *Via Media* already cited, pp. xxiv–xxv.

exercise of ministry. The lectures on the *Via Media*, a bulwark of a Catholic definition of the Church of England, were originally entitled *Lectures on the Prophetical Office of the Church Viewed Relatively to Romanism and Popular Protestantism*. The Roman Catholic preface was written for a third edition of the lectures published in 1877 as volume one of his writings on the Church of England as a reformed Catholic Church neither Roman nor Protestant. Newman considered the work as one of his five most important. The Roman Catholic preface maintains the Anglican formulation linking the Church as 'one, holy, catholic, and apostolic' with an ecclesial sharing in the three offices of Christ. But rather than use this as a base against attacks from the outside, Newman uses it to explain why the Church experiences weaknesses from the inside. Newman pointed out that while Christ exercised the three offices as Mediator, the Church shares in these offices 'in human measure'. These ministries are indivisible but diverse.[9] Their diversity and their exercise in a human way allows Newman to grant the Church a great share in the offices of Christ without at the same time divinizing the Church.

In fact, far from divinizing the Church, facing its critics, especially of the Roman Catholic Church, Newman simply says 'I begin by admitting the general truth of the facts alleged against us . . .'.[10] As we saw in his private correspondence with Lady Chatterton fourteen years previously this is typical of Newman in private, but some contemporary Roman Catholics were astonished at this public admission.[11] They were used to the more common tactic of denying allegations. And indeed, not everything being 'alleged' against the Roman Catholic Church was in fact true. Lord Acton, a Catholic scholar contemporary with Newman, was not the first nor the last historian to succumb to journalistic instincts by misreading, misquoting, and libeling Church figures (including saints).[12] Newman's own method was both more realistic and more theological. Enough historical allegations would prove true so apologetics was ultimately a waste of effort

---

[9] *Via Media*, p. 25.

[10] *Via Media*, pp. 28–9,

[11] Newman to John Rickards Mozley on 21 April 1875: 'I should say that the Church has two sides, a human and a divine, and that every thing that is human is liable to error. Whether, so considered, it has in matter of fact erred, must be determined by history, and, for the very reason that it is human as well as divine, I am disposed to believe it has, even before the fact has been proved to me by history.' *Letters and Diaries*, XXVII, Charles Stephen Dessain and Thomas Gornall, SJ (eds) (Oxford: Clarendon Press, 1975), pp. 282–3. As to the consternation of Catholics to the blunt admission see *The Month*, xii (1877), p. 373 and *Dublin Review*, ixxx (1877), pp. 514f.

[12] It was the historian Herbert Butterfield who labeled Acton's shoddy, biased work on renaissance Rome as journalistic. Newman was very critical. See Roland Hill, *Lord Acton* (Newhaven: Yale University Press, 2000), pp. 184–5, p. 449, notes 35–43.

if it tried to hold against the major proposition that there were serious wrongs done by Church officials. The real question was the theological significance of this fact. Did this fact cancel the credibility of the Church or did it point to a profound ecclesiological reality?

Now, it must be said from the first, that Newman's religious faith, especially a profound sense of Providence, was the basis for his theology. In a letter prior to writing the Preface to the third edition of the *Via Media*, Newman gives a typical outline of his confidence in Providence. His correspondent, Robert Charles Jenkins, was a church historian. Newman says to him:

> I do not look at the divisions of Christendom so very anxiously as you do, for the Catholic (i.e. the Catholic Roman) Church presents a continuous history of fearful falls and as strange and successful recoveries. We have a series of catastrophes each unlike the others, and that diversity is the pledge that the present ordeal, though different from any of the proceeding, will be overcome, in God's good time . . .

And, very relevant to our own situation, Newman went so far as to say in the face of the impending secularization he saw, 'Of course one's forecasting may be wrong – but we may be entering on quite a new course – for which the civil ignoring of Christianity may be the necessary first step, and we may have centuries of confusion – but the Church has steadily worked her way out of overwhelming misfortunes in times past, and will by God's mercy, again'.[13] Standing alone, such could be dismissed as sentiment, but the attitude had a matching theological component as well as a cool assessment of acknowledged shortcomings. It was this faith that allowed Newman to admit and confess what many would not admit and confess. Speaking of this inability to confess, Newman said many Catholics (and Christians in general?) were 'pleaders at the bar, and are afraid to make admissions lest these should be turned against them. To speak out is in the long run the wisest, the most expedient, the most noble policy; seldom the possible, or the natural'.[14] So Newman begins his search for a reformed Catholicism in a place that was seldom accessible and not natural: admitting that there was a need for Catholicism to be reformed but that deformations need not derail the fundamental value of Catholicism nor call into question the worth of searching for it.

The second aspect of Newman's theology that needs to be noted is his revision of his attack on the teaching office as peculiarly a problem. As an

---

[13] John Henry Newman, *Letters and Diaries*, XXVIII, Charles Stephen Dessain and Thomas Gornall, SJ (eds) (Oxford: Clarendon Press, 1976), p. 91.
[14] *Letters and Diaries*, XXVII, p. 265.

Anglican, Newman found the Roman teaching office prone to rationalism. This laying violent hands on the mystery of revelation offended Newman's sense of the otherness of God which theology was meant to protect. Within the Roman communion, Newman changed his mind about the dangers of Roman teaching office. A teaching office restricted by Bible and tradition, as it is not only in the Roman Church but most other churches, is not in practice very often the problem. It is the devotional or priestly office as well as the governing office that clashes most often with the sober simplicity of the teaching office. There are obvious restraints to the teaching office including the serious prohibition against introducing and imposing novelties. Most of the serious dialogue between separated Christians has been on this very point: what is essential and what is a development from the essential and what is simply novel. The novel cannot be imposed on the whole Church as something essential when the Church in the past offered salvation effectively without it. But prohibitions against the novel in devotional and governmental practice is more problematic.

In devotional matters, Newman points out, even the authority of pastors is sometimes stymied by the popularity of questionable practices. In general devotion resists novelty, but history knows waves of enthusiasm for practices that are generated in cultural interests and anxieties. These interests and anxieties have no ecclesial base at all and no theological support, but they penetrate the Church through a particular social dynamic such as the fears approaching millennia seem to produce or the fears generated by war-time conditions. Matthew 13 is especially a good pastoral rule here, since trying to eradicate these movements can do more harm than riding them out. When the priestly office favors patience, the teaching and governing offices must take a secondary role to what is obviously not theological and tending to schism or worse.

The governing office in Newman's time was for him more problematic than either the difficulties imposed by a magisterium restrained by scripture and tradition or the pastoral conundra generated by exotic devotions. In the case of the Roman curia, it was difficult to impose restraints that protected innocence by insisting on due procedures. To say that the exercise of governance was, in Newman's time, arbitrary, is to simply underscore what Protestantism still fears most about papal authority. However, the point of this paper is to remind us that all forms of governance are difficult to coordinate with pastoral and teaching ministries. Roman examples are most prominent to Newman's theology, but in his lifetime he suffered much from the governance of his own Oxford college, Oriel, under its provost and from the governance of the university, as well as from various Anglican bishops. The exercise of power is always problematic. Whether the power is centralized or decentralized does not seem to matter. Power may tend to corrupt, and absolute power tend to corrupt absolutely, but governing ministries shorn of power also tend to corruption while total lack of power tends to total corruption.

The third consideration is Newman's assertion that, while the novel is often an illegitimate and problematic reality in the exercise of the offices, a new development is not absolutely to be rejected simply on the grounds of novelty. In the *Essay on Development of Doctrine*, of course, Newman answered his old Anglican self that rejected the binding nature of further insights into revelation. History taught, he believed, that nearly all of what is acceptable in strictly orthodox theology, was a matter of development. Further, science was usually developing and the teaching office had to meet the challenge of new scientific discoveries that made some points of doctrine subject to new interpretations. In Newman's own time, politics had also challenged doctrine and many Roman theologians had to debate whether the secular authority of the Pope was necessary to papal ministry. While novel conditions do not require novel doctrines, development of doctrine might be necessary. Newman was never in favor of any doctrinal development, no matter how much he believed in it personally, if it could be avoided. Developments ought to be accepted as a last resort after their maturation.[15] Implications were always, Newman believed, difficult to foresee. A conclusion drawn quickly could solve an immediate problem but create more later. Such caution made Newman unpopular with all kinds of factions along the continuum of Christian thought and practice.

So we can conclude from Newman:

1. As long as the Church is going to function in its fullness and not as a sect, the mixed reality portrayed in Matthew 13 will be one of the signs that it bears along with unity, holiness, catholicity and apostolicity.

2. The mixed reality is often the result of the people in the Church being unequal to the coordination of the three offices entrusted to them.

3. The reality of Matthew 13 can be borne by a faith in divine providence.

4. The basis of criticism of the Church must be the same faith in providence.

5. Pastoral and doctrinal developments demanded by new situations and the need for reform and renewal must be introduced with due

---

[15] Letter to Jesuit Robert Whitty in 1870 on the eve of the controversial Vatican Council I. This council Newman thought 'inopportune'. See *Letters and Diaries*, XXV, Charles Stephen Dessain and Thomas Gornall, SJ (eds) (Oxford: Clarendon Press, 1973), pp. 92ff. For a general study of the question see John R. Page, *What Will Dr. Newman Do? John Henry Newman and Papal Infallibility, 1865–1875* (Collegeville, MN: Liturgical Press, 1994).

care. The work of reform can only be done 'without injury to what is true and good' if it is a 'gradual work. Errors of fact may do no harm, and their removal may do much'.[16]

In the light of the above, we can turn today's situation. The critical question of a Catholicism in need of reform that balked Lady Chatterton in Newman's time, was the same problem in times closer to ours. Simone Weil pushed the question to its most extreme logic when she wrote in a letter in 1942: 'Christianity should contain all vocations without exception since it is catholic. In consequence the Church should also. But in my eyes Christianity is catholic by right but not in fact . . . Christianity being catholic by right but not in fact, I regard it as legitimate on my part to be a member of the Church by right but not in fact, not only for a time, but for my whole life if need be'.[17] Simone Weil would not be alone today.

The pastoral situation of the Roman Catholic Church today is a study in the dilemma of the coordination of the three offices and the need for a reformed Catholicism. As a Church it is a good example because it alone claims not only catholicity as a doctrine, but as a corollary in administration. No other Church has tried to administratively centralize its government as has the Roman Catholic Church. This administrative centralization exists despite the fact that it has a worldwide extension of bishops all in communion with each other and within any particular country organized into national conferences. These national conferences are also organized into continental or regional bodies. If ever a Church could exercise the principle of subsidiarity and still maintain Catholic unity, it would be the Church of Rome. But the case for centralization is wonderfully illustrated by Cardinal Jorge A. Medina, Prefect of the Vatican's Congregation for Worship and Sacraments. This office is responsible for the final approval of translations for the liturgy. These translations have already been approved by the local conferences of Bishops. But this office reserves to itself the final say over translations that a one billion member church can use. How one small office in Rome would have the talent and resources necessary to judge translations and adaptations over the entire globe is hard to say. Common sense would seem to indicate that the local Bishops' Conferences would be better prepared for this kind of work. Cardinal Medina is of the opposite opinion: 'The Holy See is no stranger to any culture, not only because she lives in communion with them all, but because those who assist in her daily work come from every continent . . . And in

---

[16] *Via Media*, p. 40.
[17] Simone Weil, *Waiting for God* (New York: Harper & Row, 1951), p. 75.

the final analysis, she is the one most capable of determining whether translations faithfully transmit the content of the Latin prayers of the Roman Rite, precisely because those prayers are her own heritage, and her gift to each new generation of the faithful'.[18] This statement could conjure up a vast army of multi-lingual, multi-cultural language and liturgical experts backed up by vast library and computer databases, but the bureaucratic reality is far from that. Efficient and effective centralization in this case is a budgetary impossibility. But budgets do not get in the way of certain theologies.

More seriously, within the Roman Church, differences on the theological basis for the renewal of Catholicism now exist and can be illustrated by the argument between two Roman-based German Cardinals. Cardinal Joseph Ratzinger of the Congregation for the Doctrine of the Faith and Cardinal Walter Kasper of the Pontifical Council for the Promotion of Christian Unity have been the past few years publicly debating differing aspects of ecclesiology. Kasper's concern has been pastoral. There is a growing gap between Roman norms promulgated for the whole Catholic Church and the needs and practices of local churches. Kasper believes the practical issue is really a reflection of a larger theological one concerning the universality or catholicity of the Church. For Kasper, the Church exists at once both universally and locally. The function of the Petrine ministry is to foster the necessary diversity that true unity requires. For Cardinal Ratzinger, the universal Church is pre-existent. Therefore, for Cardinal Ratzinger, the Petrine Ministry meant for the whole Church with its preference for centralization holds the field theologically and practically. The consequences for ecumenism, says Kasper, are obvious: 'The goal of the ecumenical movement is not unity in uniformity but the existence of one church embracing peacefully a great diversity. The particular churches must remain churches, and yet more and more they must become one church'.[19]

This article began with an ideal description of catholicity by Avery Dulles (now a cardinal) and ends with a description by another theologian cardinal about the task that still needs to be done within Roman Catholicism. Newman ended his days in the Roman Catholic Church as a theologian cardinal. He had been both a critic and a victim of officials in his own church. Eventually he was vindicated and today there is serious advocacy for his canonization. Today in something of his spirit, we might suggest some directions for a clearer understanding of catholicity:

[18] Cardinal Jorge A. Medina on the ICEL Controversy, *America*, 13 May 2000, p. 19.

[19] Walter Kasper, 'On the Church, A Friendly Reply to Cardinal Ratzinger', *America*, 23–30 April 2001, pp. 13–14.

1. In ecumenical dialogue, the goal should not be the elimination of offices and powers, but their coordination. Criticism of the Roman Curia is not a criticism of the Church of Rome and its elimination is not an option. What John Paul II has asked for in his encyclical on ecumenism (*Ut Unum Sint*, 95–6) is a dialogue on the reform and execution of that ministry. Here there is plenty of scope.

2. The coordination of the offices or ministries of the Church is a question of power. Power, great or small, is loaded with ambiguity. Oppression by a majority or oppression by a central authority is still oppression. Further, our attitude towards power is ambiguous. It is one thing to criticize Pope Pius XII for allowing the German Roman Catholic Center party to be dissolved under Hitler and it is another thing to welcome a Roman Catholic political party headed by a priest into one's own country here and now. Bishops are criticized for interfering in politics when their position is disagreed with and they are criticized for not speaking up when they do not favor certain positions.

3. Decentralization for the sake of a greater catholicity is not for the sake of democratizing the Church but for a better coordination of ministry. A heavily centralized administration is inefficient and too burdensome for any one group of officials.

4. Newman's criticism of the administration of the Roman Church was based on faith and not a hermeneutics of suspicion. Such faith needs to be evident in the dialogue on catholicity.

5. On the local levels within Roman Catholic parishes, there is a greater need to act as if we were all in one Church. Whatever the theological and pastoral questions are for the worldwide Church, the local parishes have plenty of room for greater cooperation. Within Roman Catholicism, congregations are as effectively divided by Mass schedules as they would be if they were different churches. Roman Catholic parishes and institutions such as schools are often isolated from each other despite the obvious pastoral need to coordinate and share. If this is so within the reality of one Church, how much more do denominations separated from each other suffer useless duplication and division. The unity and catholicity we have now is not operational. Future progress on the international level of dialogue will not overcome or solve this local problem.

Matthew 13 is no consolation to a Church facing its critics. It is unlikely that any one program of reform will ever resolve the problems Matthew's parables dramatize. The structure of ministry seems to preclude the possibility. Catholicity, the admission and coordination of diversity, seems to disallow the purity and focus that a sect can enjoy. Newman's criticism and suffering as well as his theological contributions counsel patience. We have seen the death of utopian politics in our time. The Catholic Church needs to suffer the death of utopian theologies if it is to be Catholic.

Holiness as a Mark of the Church in the Writings of John Henry Newman

PHILIP BOYCE

THE marks or Notes are those characteristic features that distinguish the Church and help to make her recognisable as the true Church of Christ. They are normally taken to be four in number. From the sixteenth century, when Christendom was notably divided in separated Christian communities, theological treatises and studies began to expound the ways of identifying the true Church. One of those ways was through the distinguishing Notes or marks of the Church of Christ.

At first, the number of possible essential marks varied from author to author. However, by the seventeenth century, it was gradually reduced to the four Notes which take their origin from the Creed of the First Council of Constantinople in the year 381: 'I believe in the one, holy, catholic and apostolic Church'. The Church is *one* according to the will of Christ, both because there is one single Church (*uniqueness*) and because she is at one within herself (*unity*). The Church is *holy* both in what is divine in her, for example, God's presence, grace, the sacraments, etc. and also because she produces holiness in her members (*holiness*). The Church of Christ is also *Catholic* because she is sent to announce the Gospel to all peoples and races (Matt. 28:19–20), with the fullness of the means of salvation, and is not limited to any particular place, but is universal or worldwide (*catholicity*). Finally, the Church is *apostolic* because she is founded on the apostles, the foundation laid by Christ himself, and must continue to be faithful to their witness and to their teaching, making sure that she hands on the 'sound teaching' (2 Tim. 1:13) through their successors in the episcopal office (*apostolicity*).

The oldest mark of the Church, which we find ascribed to her in the most primitive baptismal symbols, is holiness. The first more structured formula of faith was the Apostles' Creed, which dates from the first two centuries of Christianity. It summarises the teaching of the Apostles and was used as a profession of faith in the Church of Rome. It says: 'I believe in . . . the holy Catholic Church, the communion of saints, the forgiveness of sins . . .'.

Holiness was an attribute of which the early Christians were keenly aware: they were called to a stricter moral code; they had martyrs in their ranks; they shared in the Eucharist; they looked forward to a life of fulfilment and union with God hereafter, and while on earth they believed that they had been chosen out of this world 'to be holy and blameless before God in love' (Eph. 1:4). Even the assembly to which they belonged, the *ekklesia*, reminded them of being set apart as 'citizens with the saints', called to grow 'into a holy temple in the Lord' (Eph. 2:19, 21).

When we speak of the Church as being holy, it is obvious that our experience will immediately tell us that many things seem to contradict this statement. In fact, it cannot be denied that saints and sinners make up the Church, that human weakness and sinfulness tarnish the beauty of the Church and impair her witnessing power. Even her holiest rites begin with an acknowledgment of sin and a plea for mercy.

There exists side by side in the Church the divine and the human element. For the most part, one is invisible, the other visible and open to human scrutiny. What is meant by saying that the Church is holy is that in her divine aspect and deepest essence, as the Body of Christ and Temple of the Holy Spirit, she is truly holy, while her human members and institutions share in varying degrees, depending on time and circumstances, in that essential holiness.

Objectively, the Church is holy because she is separated from the profane and belongs to God. She is always united with Christ whose presence and sacramental grace continuously sanctify her members. Loved by God and purified in Christ's Passion, she has been given all the means of sanctification – the sacraments, the revealed truths, the ordained ministries. Her members who are baptised were from the beginning called 'saints' (cf. Acts 9:13). The Dogmatic Constitution on the Church of the Second Vatican Council affirms:

> The Church . . . is held, as a matter of faith, to be unfailingly holy. This is because Christ, the Son of God, who with the Father and the Spirit is hailed as 'alone holy', loved the Church as his Bride, giving himself up for her so as to sanctify her (cf. Eph. 5:25–26); he joined her to himself as his body and endowed her with the gift of the Holy Spirit for the glory of God. Therefore, all in the Church, whether they belong to the hierarchy or are

cared for by it, are called to holiness, according to the apostle's saying: 'For this is the will of God, your sanctification' (1 Thess. 4:3; cf. Eph. 1:4).[1]

The final sentence of this quotation refers to the subjective or personal holiness that should follow as a result of the Church's objective holiness springing from her association with what is divine. This ethical progress to holiness in her members is something that is forever underway in this world and never completely attained until the members reach 'the heavenly Jerusalem'. Therefore, even in the human part of the Church, the holiness of her members is 'real though imperfect'.[2] There are the saints; there are countless acts of charity, self-sacrifice, faithfulness, patience in suffering, fidelity to the faith even amid persecution, missionary proclamation and heroic virtue. There are also sinners, and most sins, even grievous ones, do not separate a person from the Church. Hence, 'the Church clasping sinners to her bosom, at once holy and always in need of purification, follows constantly the path of penance and renewal'.[3]

The life of John Henry Newman – born 200 years ago, 21 February 1801 – was dominated by the Church, which in one form or another constantly shaped the web of his existence. The Church of Christ was for him the object of his dearest hopes and most generous undertakings, the source of unsuspected grace and joy, while at the same time the cause of deep anxiety, prolonged search, keen suffering and heart-breaking decisions. On the ecclesial Community which he believed, at various periods of his spiritual journey, to be the true Church of Christ, he lavished his best energies and talents, and accepted the most demanding sacrifices.

In a detailed reply to Charles Kingsley's accusations, Newman gives the following description of the 'Notes of the Church': 'Certain great and simple characteristics, which He who founded the Church has stamped upon her in order to draw both the reason and the imagination of men to her, as being really a divine work, and a religion distinct from all other religious communities; the principal of these Notes being that she is Holy, One, Catholic, and Apostolic, as the Creed says'.[4] We are now interested in particular in the Note of holiness.

Word and sacrament

Christ's intention in founding his Church was to save souls and lead them to perfection. He brings them into his Church not merely to make them

---

[1] Vatican II, *Lumen Gentium*, No. 39. For a survey of the origin and contents of the theology of the marks of the Church, cf. Gustav Thils, *Les Notes de l'église dans l'apologétique catholique depuis la réforme* (Brussels: Gembloux, 1937).

[2] Vatican II, *Dogmatic Constitution on the Church*, L.G., No. 48.

[3] Ibid., No. 8.

[4] *Apologia pro vita sua*. Martin I. Svaglic (ed.) (Oxford: Clarendon Press, 1967), p. 437.

orderly citizens of society but rather 'citizens with the saints and members of the household of God' (Eph. 2:19). The aim of the divine talents given to her is to foster holiness in the baptised.

Baptism is the sacrament that initiates the process of holiness in the lives of Christians. It is a basic component of the mark of holiness in the Church, especially if we consider the ideal of justification Newman professed and the radical change it involves in the spiritual nature of the believer. It is true that Newman in his first preaching did tend to Calvinistic ideas about the division of the world into converted and unconverted. However, under the influence of Edward Hawkins, the evangelical Vicar of St Mary's at the time, he changed his mind. By January of 1825, he was convinced of the necessity of an inward change, a regeneration through sacramental grace, as can be noted from an entry in an early Journal: 'It seems to me that the great stand is to be made, *not* against those who connect a spiritual change with baptism, but against those who deny a spiritual change altogether'.[5]

Justification is both a blotting out of sin and a renewal or transformation of the soul. In itself the change is but one simple action, yet we can make a mental distinction between its two parts: pardon and renewal. It can be compared to a ray of sunshine flashing into a dark room: the one act both dispels the dimness and floods the room with light. 'In like manner', says Newman, 'there is, in fact, no middle state between a state of *wrath* and a state of *holiness*. In justifying, God takes away what is past, *by* bringing in what is new. He snatches us out of the fire by lifting us in His everlasting hands, and enwrapping us in His own glory.'[6]

Newman was emphatic in maintaining that the pardon granted by God is real. When God, in his goodness, declares the sinner righteous in justification, his word effects what it proclaims. No part of the soul is left untouched, unsanctified. It implies making and not simply counting a person to be righteous. A person is renewed from within and is made pleasing and acceptable to God: 'Justification renews, therefore, I say it may fitly be called renewal . . . And we might of course with property urge that baptism is not a mere outward rite, but an inward power; and so we may say that *justification* is a *change of heart*'.[7]

From his reading of Scripture, Newman came to the conviction that the deeply sanctifying cause of all that baptismal regeneration means was

---

[5] *Autobiographical Writings,* edited with Introductions by Henry Tristram of the Oratory (London and New York: Sheed & Ward, 1956), p. 78.

[6] *Lectures on the Doctrine of Justification* (London: Longmans, Green & Co., 1908), p. 102.

[7] Ibid., pp. 86, 88. Cf. Thomas L. Sheridan, *Newman on Justification* (New York: Alba House, 1967), pp. 239–65.

ultimately the divine presence within the soul in grace. Indeed, the great gift of the Gospel, the inward reality that transforms and deifies, 'is nothing short of the indwelling in us of God the Father and the Word Incarnate through the Holy Ghost. If this be so, we have found what we sought: *This* is to be justified, to receive the Divine Presence within us, and be made a Temple of the Holy Ghost'.[8]

This is Newman's conclusion at the end of his study on Justification, a conclusion which offers a possible meeting ground for the different schools of Christian thought. More than to faith itself (in Protestant thought) or to a renovating, supernatural quality imparted by grace (in Roman Catholic thought), he went back to the role of uncreated grace. He tried to make the discordant views converge in the presence of the Divine Persons in the soul who produce both faith and the renovating quality in the soul.[9] In Newman's opinion, it was the very presence of the Trinity itself (not merely through grace) that gave dignity to justified souls and added splendour to the holiness of the Church. Years later, as a Roman Catholic, he would express this thought to a correspondent who queried him about the Presence of the Holy Spirit in the tongues of fire that fell upon the Apostles at Pentecost:

> . . . As to the *invisible grace*. In these later times it is usual to say that the Third Person of the Blessed Trinity resides in the soul by means of His *grace* – but it is still a theological opinion maintained by great divines (and I suspect the old opinion) that His Presence in the soul is not merely His grace but *Himself*. I should say the same here. The descent of the Holy Spirit upon the Apostles may be understood of His actual Personal Presence in their souls, or of a special grace making them and qualifying them to be Apostles.[10]

Holiness as a mark of the Church implies that she has the effective means of sanctifying. Newman always considered these means to be, above all, the Sacraments. We have briefly sketched his teaching on the sanctifying power of baptism. The same is true, in its appropriate fashion, for each of the other sacraments. Contrasting them with the Jewish ordinances of old, Newman illustrated their superior power:

> . . . Christ shines through them, as through transparent bodies, without impediment. He is the Light and Life of the Church, acting through it, dispensing of His fulness, knitting and compacting together every part of it;

---

[8] *Lectures on the Doctrine of Justification*, p. 144.

[9] Cf. C. Stephen Dessain, 'Cardinal Newman and the Doctrine of Uncreated Grace': *The Clergy Review* 47 (1962), pp. 207–25, 269–88.

[10] *The Letters and Diaries of John Henry Newman*, edited at the Birmingham Oratory. Vols XI–XXII (London: Nelson, 1961–72); Vols XXIII–XXXI; I–VII (Oxford: Clarendon Press 1973–95). Still in progress. Vol. XXIV, p. 144.

and these its mysteries are not merely outward signs, but (as it were) effluences of His grace developing themselves in external forms.[11]

What baptism initiates, the Eucharist nourishes and develops. Newman was always devoted to the Sacrament of the Eucharist. From Hurrell Froude he learned the doctrine on the Real Presence during the Eucharistic banquet. As an Anglican, he also believed in the sacrificial aspect of the Mass, without however admitting the doctrine of transubstantiation.[12] Central to his spiritual teaching was the Holy Eucharist – an indispensable means of acquiring holiness.

As a Roman Catholic, Newman displayed an even more tender devotion to the Real Presence, also in the Reserved Sacrament. It became a sustaining source of comfort and unifying power with Christ. Four months after his reception, he writes to Henry Wilberforce from the Seminary at Maryvale:

> I am writing next to the Chapel – It is such an incomprehensible blessing to have Christ in bodily presence in one's house, within one's walls, as swallows up all other privileges and destroys, or should destroy, every pain. To know that He is close by – to be able again and again through the day to go in to Him . . . It is *the* place for intercession, surely, where the Blessed Sacrament is.[13]

As well as through the power of the sacraments, the Church of Christ also has the divinely-given commission to sanctify through the preaching of the Word. Newman was keenly aware from the beginning of his clerical career of his grave responsibility to transmit the Gospel as a minister of Christ and of the Church. When taking up his new duties of tutorship in Oriel College, he wrote in his Journal: 'May I engage in them in the strength of Christ, remembering that I am a minister of God, and have a commission to preach the Gospel, remembering the worth of souls and that I have to answer for the opportunities given me of benefitting those who are under my care.[14]

Newman effaced himself before the sacred text which he preached. He spoke, not to gain popularity, but for the purpose of making his listeners better friends of Christ. Like Thomas Scott, his motto would be: 'holiness

---

[11] *Parochial and Plain Sermons*, 8 Volumes (London: Longmans, Green & Co., 1908–11), Vol. III, pp. 272–8.

[12] Cf. *Newman the Oratorian*. His unpublished Oratory Papers, edited with an Introductory Study on the continuity between his Anglican and his Catholic Ministry by Placid Murray, OSB (Dublin: Gill & Macmillan Ltd, 1969), pp. 43–58; *Apologia pro vita sua* (Svaglic (ed.)), pp. 33–5.

[13] *The Letters and Diaries*, XI, p. 129.

[14] *Autobiographical Writings*, p. 209.

rather than peace'.[15] He put forward a high moral standard of living and exhorted people to newness of life. He preached the truth believing in its power to prevail.

Accordingly, the mark of holiness involved, according to Newman, that the Church should possess the effective means of sanctification, notably the sacraments and the preaching of the revealed word of truth in its entirety, which has the power to save. Another question came painfully into Newman's life, namely, do these Notes and specifically the mark of holiness, identify the true Church of Christ?

Holiness, a mark of identification

To say that the Church of Christ has four essential marks that help to distinguish her does not mean that one can demonstrate the true Church by means of them. To profess the true Church, one must receive a special grace and follow the call of conscience. Moreover, some of these Notes may not be exclusive to her: they may be shared in varying degrees by different Christian traditions. Taken together, however, the four Notes or marks have a cogent force and persuasive power.

By the year 1840, Newman and some of his Tractarian friends were becoming more and more unhappy with certain trends in the Church of England at that time. It seemed to them that she did not assert her moral authority and freedom from the State in matters religious. A final instance of compromise took place in 1841. It was a question of a bishopric which the Anglican Church wished to set up in Jerusalem in conjunction with the Lutheran Church of Prussia. Each Church would nominate in turn a bishop who would have jurisdiction over all Protestants living in the area as well as over some heretical congregations of the Middle East. The Prussian Church did not even have bishops, it was non-episcopalian; hence all candidates for the see would be consecrated by Anglican Bishops. It seemed clear to Newman that it was a compromise on a doctrinal issue for the sake of political prestige in the Middle East. Such 'fraternising' which infringed Church discipline in a serious matter and ignored her doctrine was more than he could tolerate. An unsigned letter to the Editor of *The Times*, which in the event was never published, was charged with bitter irony. 'Surely, it is an evil great enough to find Bishops heretics, without going on to make heretics Bishops.'[16]

---

[15] *Apologia pro vita sua* (Svaglic (ed.)), p. 19.

[16] Letter to the Editor of *The Times*, 10 October 1841, quoted in Ian Ker, *John Henry Newman: A Biography* (Oxford and New York: Oxford University Press, 1988), p. 235.

Newman's theory of the *Via Media* fell apart. He could no longer see how the Anglican Church was an integral part of the *One* Church, without by the same token arguing in favour of the corruptions he considered to exist in the Roman system. At the very least, he considered the Church of his birth to be 'in an abnormal state'. At the same time, this did not justify him in leaving his own ecclesial Communion. He felt his old 'objections against Rome as strongly as ever' and he knew he could not go against his conscience. The latter was a higher rule than any argument about the Notes of the Church.[17]

Nevertheless, his final despairing appeal to those who were tempted to secede to Rome rested on the mark of holiness which he considered still to be an evident possession of the Church of England. He called it the 'Note of Life', the Note of Christ's Presence in the lives of good Anglicans. It was not any sort of life, 'but a supernatural Christian life which could only come directly from above'.[18] He had recourse to this argument repeatedly during these years, notably in a famous article entitled 'The Catholicity of the Anglican Church' in The *British Critic* of January 1841; shortly afterwards in *Tract 90* and, in particular, in four sermons delivered during the final two months of 1841.[19]

Newman attaches great importance to this Note: it is apologetic, evangelising, persuasive. It is the true test of a Church. Life draws others to follow; mere words simply fly in the wind. 'Much as Roman Catholics may denounce us at present as schismatical, they could not resist us, if the Anglican communion had but that one Note of the Church upon it . . . sanctity.'[20]

One is reminded of some Fathers of the Church who appealed for a sincere Christian life on account of its apostolic value. St John Chrysostom asserted that 'there would be no need for words, if we manifested works. There would be no gentile, if we were true Christians'.[21] And centuries later, St Bernard stated that 'a false Catholic does much more harm than if a true heretic were to appear'.[22]

Another reason why Newman attached so much importance to the Note of sanctity at this time, was that he seemed surer of his ground in attacking

---

[17] *Apologia pro vita sua* (Svaglic (ed.)), p. 139.

[18] Ibid., p. 140.

[19] The article in the *British Critic* was published in *Essays Critical and Historical* (London: Longmans, Green & Co., 1910), Vol. II, pp. 1–73; the four sermons in *Sermons on Subjects of the Day* (London: Longmans, Green & Co., 1909), pp. 308–80.

[20] *Essays Critical and Historical*, Vol. II, p. 69, and *Apologia pro vita sua*, p. 150.

[21] *Commentary on 1 Tim.* Homily 10: Migne, *Patrologia Graeca*, Vol. 62, Col. 551.

[22] *Commentary on the Canticle of Canticles*, Sermon 65,5: Migne, *Patrologia Latina*, Vol. 183, Col. 1091D.

Roman Catholics. This Note did not compel him to confront and refute Roman doctrines or even popular beliefs, where he found himself on unsure ground. In the case of sanctity of life, he felt he could not be refuted and that he could not be mistaken.

> For what is a higher guide for us in speculation and in practice, than that conscience of right and wrong, of truth and falsehood, those sentiments of what is decorous, consistent, and noble, which our Creator has made a part of our original nature? Therefore I felt I could not be wrong in attacking what I fancied was a fact, – the unscrupulousness, the deceit, and the intriguing spirit of the agents and representatives of Rome.[23]

Newman continued to grapple bravely with this Note of sanctity to which he attributed so much importance in those years. In the article on English Catholicity that appeared in January of 1840 in the *British Critic*, he had, as he confessed to Keble, 'almost shot his last arrow against Rome'.[24] There he had begun to stress the value of holiness and goodness of life, which, he intimated, outweighed the faults and deficiencies of being separated from the general body of the Church. He gave the example of St Melitus in the fourth century who for a while was suspected of being a semi-Arian and consequently lost the favour of Pope Damasus and of St Athanasius. However, being a saintly man, he was later reinstated. Newman pointed to his 'meekness, gentleness, sweetness of temper and generosity of feeling' as qualities that made up for his separation from Rome and Alexandria and 'prove that saints may be matured in a state which Romanists of this day would fain call schism'.[25] The same held true of the Anglican Communion about which he himself and some of his congregation were beginning to have doubts. The Note of sanctity seemed to give stability and assurance when other marks were failing.

After the rejection of *Tract 90* by Church authorities and the unholy alliance in the bishopric affair in Jerusalem, Newman felt that the mark of Apostolic succession and the fulness of primitive doctrine were impaired. Then, as we mentioned, he had recourse to the inward signs of holiness and divine grace that still existed among many good Anglicans. If his Church could produce such effects in the lives of believers, surely God must still be with her and she must surely be still pleasing to him. He

---

[23] *Apologia* (Svaglic (ed.)), pp. 140–1. 'And till Roman Catholics renounce political efforts, and manifest in their public measures the light of holiness and truth, perpetual war is our only prospect' (ibid., p. 141).

[24] Cf. *Letters and Diaries*, VII, p. 418.

[25] *Essays Critical and Historical*, Vol. II, p. 65. So much did he value the Note of Sanctity that he even stated that if Rome were to reform its ways, it would be his 'Church's duty at once to join in communion with the Continental Churches' (ibid., p. 72).

compared Anglicanism to Samaria. Although the Ten Tribes of the Jewish People were separated from the Tribe of Judah and the holy City of Jerusalem, they still had prophets (such as Elijah and Elisha) sent to them, they still had holy people in their ranks and still had the means of grace and acceptance despite the outward separation. Similarly, God's life was evident in the Anglican Communion. In this way he tried to reassure doubting Anglicans.

Newman was not speaking to those who were undisturbed in their religious convictions, nor did he address those who were restless because they had not practised their religion with any depth or consistency. But for others – and for himself – who witnessed the external, objective signs of ecclesial authenticity becoming weak, he turned in his preaching to the subjective presence of Christ that produced holiness of life. Here he found consolation and reassurance:

> How great a blessing is it, my brethren, at all times, but especially in an age like this, that the tokens of Christ are not only without us, but more properly within us! I say in this age especially, because it is an age in which the outward signs of Christ's Presence have well nigh deserted us . . . Since then, in this our age, He has in judgement obscured the visible and public Notes of His kingdom among us: what a mercy is it to us that He has not deprived us of such as are personal and private![26]

This was the first time that this renowned preacher brought into the pulpit his personal problems with Anglicanism and the doubts of a number of his congregation who had started since the beginning of that year (1841) to secede to Rome. He pointed specifically to their experience of God's presence and grace in holy places, at the reception of the Holy Sacrament or at the Rite of Ordination, at providential events of life or in the peace surrounding a holy deathbed. Such experiences should reassure them that God was still giving grace through their Church services and ordinances. In this sense, he entreated the wavering listeners among his audience: 'O! pause ere you doubt that we have a Divine Presence among us still, and have not to seek it . . . And we will cling to the Church in which we are, not for its own sake, but because we humbly trust that Christ is in it; and while He is in it, we will abide in it'.[27]

Newman did understand that this subjective approach was fraught with danger. It was an abandoning of the more objective *Via Media* in favour of a subjective reliance on personal religious experiences. Some of his best friends were deeply perplexed. In their eyes, he was substituting 'a sort of methodistic self-contemplation' for the objective Notes and tokens, 'as

---

[26] *Sermons bearing on Subjects of the Day*, p. 318.
[27] Ibid., pp. 322–3.

they were commonly received, of a divine presence in the Anglican Church'.[28] In fact, subjective experience, even of a divine presence, can only be an added affirmation to what is clear through objective and ecclesial tokens. God always authenticated the truth in this way. Even Paul the Apostle, despite the overwhelming conviction of what he experienced on the road to Damascus, had to get objective confirmation by others to whom he was directed by the heavenly vision (cf. Acts 9:3–19).

Newman himself soon began to find his position untenable. The very theory he preached in order to reassure his listeners began to dissatisfy himself. He would later admit it to be specious to look upon but difficult to prove and work. He did everything, short of disobeying his conscience, to avert his secession. At last, he arranged for a Passionist Father, a missionary in England, who was passing through Oxford, to break his journey and visit Littlemore. There he was received into the Roman Catholic Church.

It is easy to gloss over the event and not consider what was, humanly speaking, the tragic nature of Newman's decision. He felt he was letting down many friends and admirers. In some ways he suffered an irreparable loss. He knew however that he could not disobey the light and the call he received. As we contemplate him, it is neither a feeling of triumphalistic satisfaction or sad disappointment that is uppermost in our heart, but one of awe at the sight of an upright man making a heart-rending decision, not urged by any human consideration or gain but guided purely by the light of conscience and duty. This we have to admire.

Newman had always looked upon the Church as the custodian of revealed truth and the embodiment of sanctity. He now recognised the Church of Rome as faithful to her founding Master and loyal to the principles of Antiquity. She had divinely-instituted means of sanctification and, despite certain appearances, did produce holiness among her members. She had the spiritual power and courage to demand holiness of life, heroic devotion, undaunted sacrifice. Following the ideals set forth in the New Testament, she recoiled from compromise, censured mediocrity and pursued Christian perfection.

This point was made honestly, albeit sadly, by friends of his and eminent members of the Church of England at the time. William Lake, Dean of Durham, who had always admired the famous Oxford preacher, in a letter to *The Guardian* a few weeks after Newman's death, asserts that his defection also proved to be a stimulus to the Anglican Communion to embark on a renewal of life.

> I take this devotion to the highest ideal of Christian and Church life in its absolute reality to have been the predominant feature in Cardinal Newman,

---

[28] *Apologia pro vita sua* (Svaglic (ed.)), p. 145.

which must always be his characteristic in the eyes of religious men . . . But surely this high ideal of a living Church, in its reality and its power, is among the best memorials that he has bequeathed to us. He left us because he could not then find it amongst us. He had tried the Church of England, as it then was, as the Church of 'Evangelicalism', the Church of Whately or of Hawkins, the Church of the '*Via Media*' and the Apostolic succession. All these had failed him. The one thing he craved for, and, alas! could not then find, was that the Church of England was the Church of the highest devotion and self-sacrifice . . . Has this defect in any respect been remedied since? I believe it has, and that it is to Newman even more than to his fellow-workers that we owe it – to the power and beauty of his life and writings, and even to the manner in which he pointed out our defects. In all these points, it is not too much to call him the founder of 'the Church of England as we see it'.[29]

The respected Dean Church, of St Paul's, a friend who was much closer to Newman than was Dean Lake, had expressed similar considerations just a few days after the Cardinal's death in a noble tribute which appeared also in *The Guardian*. He too sees the criterion of truth for Newman in the ideals of the New Testament. Not that the Cardinal approved of Anglicans joining the Church of Rome simply because they found or hoped to find there more scope for fervour and devotion. The decision to move had to rest on the discovery of truth and the call of conscience, although devotion and fervour, resting on doctrinal truth, had their necessary place. It was the Note of sanctity, which Newman at last discovered in the Church of Rome that was to be the final thrust leading him to change his ecclesial allegiance:

> Is not the ultimate key to Newman's history his keen and profound sense of the life, society, and principles of action preserved in the New Testament . . . The English Church had exchanged religion for civilisation, the first century for the nineteenth . . . at least the Roman Church had not only preserved, but maintained at full strength through the centuries to our day two things of which the New Testament was full, and which are characteristic of it – devotion and self-sacrifice . . . Devotion and self-sacrifice, prayer and self-denying charity, in one word sanctity, are at once on the surface of the New Testament and interwoven with all its substance. He recoiled from a representation of the New Testament which to his eye was without them. He turned to where, in spite of every other disadvantage, he thought he found them. In S. Filippo Neri he could find a link between the New Testament and progressive civilisation. He could find no S. Filippo – so modern yet so scriptural – when he sought at home.[30]

[29] Letter by Dean Lake to *The Guardian*, 27 August 1890, and Katherine Lake (ed.), *Memorials of William Charles Lake* (London: E. Arnold, 1901), p. 302.

[30] *The Guardian*, 13 August 1890. Cf. R. W. Church, *Occasional Papers* (London and New York: Macmillan, 1897), Vol. II, pp. 470–4.

The Note of sanctity, then, did play an important role in Newman's d 
cernment of the Church of Christ. By itself, it would not suffice to determin 
the validity of a Church's claim, but it is an essential feature of the true
Church. For the five years preceding his reception into the Church of Rome,
it was significantly and poignantly crucial for him.

The call to holiness

A final point we wish to mention briefly is the holiness that belongs to the
Church of Christ in so far as she obliges her members to strive for Christian
perfection, and has the effective power to save and sanctify them. She is
aware that she is a 'communion of saints'. This is a sharing in holy things
by holy people. The riches of Christ's grace are granted freely to all believers
especially through their union in faith and charity, through the grace of
the sacraments and the special gifts or charisms given by the Spirit to
individuals in order to benefit and strengthen the whole Body of Christ.
As the celebrant proclaims in certain Eastern liturgies, at the elevation of
the gifts: 'Holy gifts for God's holy people' (*Sancta sanctis!*).

Newman firmly rejected at all times the compromise put forward by a
well-to-do class who, fearing any excess in religious and devotional
practices, promoted the idea that the principal task of a Christian Church
was to produce 'good members of society, honest, upright, industrious and
well-conducted'.[31]

The true scriptural Church, he argues, is not simply the one that produces
the decent gentleman, the *mere* gentleman. Education by itself would not
noticeably reduce crime and sin, making people more religious and
observant. If that were the case, the Church could glory in much numerical
success. But she aims at a higher perfection, for which the multitude do
not readily strive: 'the great object of her Sacraments, preaching, Scriptures,
and instructions, is to save the elect of God, to foster into life and rear up
into perfection what is really good, not in the sight of man merely, but
what is true and holy'.[32]

Holiness is a mark of the Church because, in her human element, she is
made up of saints who are heroically dedicated, and of many others who

---

[31] *Parochial and Plain Sermons*, Vol. IV, p. 160. 'They put aside all such hungering and
thirsting after righteousness as visionary, high-flown, and what they call romantic. They
have a certain definite and clear view of their duties; they think that the summit of perfection
is to be decent and respectable in their calling, to enjoy moderately the pleasures of life, to
eat and drink, and marry and give in marriage, and buy and sell, and plant and build, and to
take care that religion does not *engross* them. Alas! and is it so? Is the supernatural life
enjoined on us in the Gospel but a dream?' (ibid., pp. 165–6).

[32] Ibid., p. 161.

striving for holiness of life. Newman never accepted any watered-down version of perfection. He understood that the Church, in meeting with the world, cannot tolerate unfaithfulness to her Master's ideals or any sort of compromise.

During the course of his life, Newman always placed before his listeners the ideal of a supernatural holiness to which they were obliged as baptised members of the Church. This was the purpose that inspired the Oxford Movement. While it undoubtedly aimed at freeing the Church from the shackles of the state and making it aware of its own divine authority, it looked beyond that to a spiritual renewal of the Church, both clerical and lay. It refused to be satisfied with the correctness that could be acquired through any philosophical ethics or utilitarian considerations. 'The Tractarians sought a renewed awareness of transcendent mystery and a renewed sense of human life as guided by a transcendent power to a transcendent goal.'[33] In other words, they tried to raise the level of Christian living beyond the common mediocrity to an ideal of holiness that was founded on baptismal grace and nurtured by the Sacraments and the practice of virtue as demanded by the Gospel.

Grace, Newman realised, was a living and dynamic reality, a divine 'seed' destined to grow into a thing of superior beauty and unsuspected holiness: 'As the seed has a tree within it, so men have within them Angels. Hence the great stress laid in Scripture on growing in grace. Seeds are intended to grow into trees. We are regenerated in order that we may be renewed daily after the Image of Him who has regenerated us'.[34] The ontological sanctity of baptismal righteousness postulates, as its natural issue, the holiness of the whole person, with all his thoughts and actions. It is meant to penetrate his faculties and influence his conduct. The tiniest degree of holiness has within it the tendency to greater holiness and to perfect sanctity.[35]

The law of dynamic growth and progressive development makes the earnest Christian a person who is forever striving for something that is beyond him, going beyond the 'already' to the 'not yet' attained. Some got the impression that Newman demanded too much: 'You give us no alternative . . . except that of being sinners or Saints'.[36] He did not withdraw

---

[33] Eugene R. Fairweather (ed.), *The Oxford Movement* (Oxford University Press, 1964), p. 5.

[34] *Parochial and Plain Sermons*, Vol. V, p. 351.

[35] Cf. Philip Boyce, OCD, 'Holiness – the Purpose of Life according to Newman': Günter Biemer und Heinrich Fries (eds), *Christliche Heiligkeit als Lehre und Praxis nach John Henry Newman*, Newman Studien, XII (Sigmaringendorf: Regio Verlag Glock und Lutz, 1988), pp. 136–47.

[36] *Discourses Addressed to Mixed Congregations*, p. 117. Cf. pp. 119–22.

his demands, but simply drew a distinction between various *kinds* of sanctity, as well as pointing out that each person has to acquire his/her own personal holiness and not imitate the saints in a slavish manner.

The saints, in particular the canonised models, display the power of holiness that the Church possesses. Missionaries, religious and martyrs are visible witnesses to the mark of holiness in the Church of Christ. The supreme model is Saint Mary, the mother of Jesus. With a title that some find difficult to understand, she is venerated by Roman Catholics as the Immaculate Conception. Newman did not openly profess this doctrine until he entered the Church of Rome – although personally he did not seem to have difficulty with it and was even accused on one occasion after an Anglican sermon of secretly holding it.[37]

The premises for such a belief were his high regard for Mary as the Mother of the Incarnate Son of God. He saw how fitting it was for a person who was so near God to be completely free of sin. Above all, from his Patristic readings, he learned they make much of the parallel between Eve and Mary: if Eve was sinless on the day she was created, it seemed appropriate that Mary should be equally free from sin at the dawn of a new creation.

Such was Newman's teaching on holiness as a mark of the Church. It was always a most significant and life-giving feature for him. At one period of his life it became poignantly important for him and seemed to outweigh in value other ecclesial Notes. But to some degree, sanctity can be and is a feature of all Churches and ecclesial Communions. It must therefore be judged together with other marks or Notes.

Moreover, unlike other Notes, it can vary in intensity, if we consider the human component of the Church: 'Sanctity admits of *degrees*, unity does not admit of degrees. The Church may be more or less holy – she cannot be more or less *one*',[38] he explains to a correspondent.

However, it was an all-important mark of the Church for Newman. He spent his life advocating and reinforcing it in the Communions to which he belonged at different periods of his life. To the Church of Rome he came as to 'the Mother of Saints'[39] and the nurturer of holiness.

---

[37] The passage that gave offence and roused suspicion was from a sermon preached on the Feast of the Annunciation, 1832: 'Who can estimate the holiness and perfection of her, who was chosen to be the Mother of Christ? . . . This contemplation runs to a higher subject, did we dare follow it; for what, think you, was the sanctified state of that human nature, of which God formed His sinless Son; knowing as we do, "that which is born of the flesh is flesh," and that "none can bring a clean thing out of an unclean?"' (*Parochial and Plain Sermons*, Vol. II, pp. 131–2.) He seemed to his listeners to imply that Mary's human nature had always been in a sanctified state of grace, hence always without sin.

[38] *The Letters and Diaries*, XV, p. 152.

[39] *Discourses Addressed to Mixed Congregations*, p. 232.

Phronesis, Development and Doctrinal Definition

DAVID BROWN

WHAT I would like to do in this article is explore the relation between doctrinal definition on the one hand and on the other two of Newman's most characteristic emphases: the idea of development and the need for practical wisdom or *phronesis*. The idea of development, he contends, makes definition more appropriate in one historical epoch than another, while practical wisdom is needed to decide when that point has been reached. Although in so doing I hope to cast some light on various tensions in Newman's thought, my primary intention is not historical. Rather, it is to explore where we might be said to stand today, and thus the kind of difference made by another century or more of change in the Church. As illustration, the central part of this essay will focus on the fate of two doctrines that reached a decisive phase in their development in the years 1853–4. If the 8th of December 1854 witnessed an expansion of dogma with Pius IX's decree on the immaculate conception, the dismissal of F. D. Maurice from his professorial chair in November of the previous year for denying hell as a place of eternal punishment can be seen as a decisive move in the opposite direction, the unravelling of a hitherto universally held Christian belief.[1] Superficially, of course, the two issues might be said just to concern their respective denominations. In fact, however, as his correspondence with Newman on the matter makes

---

[1] Partly because of the status of the person questioning the belief – one of the country's leading theologians – and partly because of the lukewarmness of his condemnation – only fifteen out of a possible forty-two turned up to the meeting that effected his condemnation: so O. Chadwick, *The Victorian Church* (London: SCM Press, 1971), I, p. 548, n. 3. The pull the other way is perhaps more clearly indicated in the 11,000 clergy who protested at the denial of the doctrine, seven years later, in *Essay and Reviews*.

clear, the papal pronouncement was one key factor in keeping Pusey an Anglican, while a century on and even the present pope's favourite theologian, Hans Urs von Balthasar, can be found espousing views not all that dissimilar to those of Maurice. When one adds to that the existence of a number of interconnections between the two doctrines, then the case for taking these cases as significant becomes in my view compelling. Whether the reader agrees will need to wait my subsequent discussion. In the meantime I want to begin by first clarifying Newman's own position on doctrinal definition in general.

Newman's general position

In declaring that 'the Fathers made me a Catholic' Newman was drawing attention to the way in which on his view his patristic studies had led naturally and inevitably to his conversion,[2] but in applying the Vincentian canon (*semper, ubique et ab omnibus*) as an Anglican he was of course doing nothing new. The appeal to ecumenical councils and to the life of the early Church had long been pursued with varying degrees of enthusiasm.[3] Although more of a natural controversialist than Pusey, like Pusey Newman was not concerned to force a particular reading of the Anglican position, but rather, more weakly, to insist that Anglican formularies were consonant with such a reading. When the response to *Tract 90* appeared to disclose that even that much was not permitted, the change was perhaps inevitable,[4] but it is doubtful whether on its own it would have forced the change (Pusey after all remained), had his earlier studies of Arianism and other major disputes in the early Church not disclosed a worrying complication in this appeal to universal positions: that the Church was sometimes found acting against the dissent of either a present majority or else a previously established consensus. Hence the importance of Augustine's words: '*securus iudicat orbis terrarum*', for in those words, as Newman memorably puts it, 'Antiquity was deciding against itself'.[5] The Donatists in their dispute with Augustine had past practice and St Cyprian on their side, but that was not enough. In other words, the authority of the present Church and its

[2] *Certain Difficulties Felt by Anglicans* (1891), II, p. 24.

[3] Ken and Van Mildert took the first eight centuries, Hammond and Stillingfleet a century less, while Jewell and Cosin retreated one century more.

[4] Cf. *Via Media* II, p. 265 (part of the 1877 Preface to *Tract 90*).

[5] This quotation and the ones which immediately follow are in fact all from the *Apologia* (London: Fontana, 1959), p. 184. Although not translated there, two translations are offered elsewhere: 'the Christian commonwealth judges without misgiving (*Letters and Diaries*, XXIV, p. 354); 'the whole church has no chance of being wrong' (ibid., XXV, p. 220). The original context is Augustine's *Contra epistolam Parmeniani* 3.4.24 (PL 43:101).

consensus needs sometimes to be set against its past positions, and how that can be possible is of course the question to which the *Essay on Development* is the intended answer. What was required was a 'deliberate judgement, in which the whole Church at length rests and acquiesces'; then one could speak of 'an infallible prescription and a final sentence'.

Although occasional attempts are still made to apply the *Essay's* seven 'notes' or tests of development,[6] it is widely acknowledged that the argument of the work as a whole fares much better, in forcing the Church towards recognition of the fact of development rather than in offering any very precise conception of how this proceeds. Indeed, further research into Newman's position discloses how deeply conservative some of his assumptions surprisingly were. In particular, one observes how as a way of maintaining continuity he was even prepared to retain some kind of implicit knowledge for earlier strands of the tradition, no matter what strains this might impose on what could possibly be meant. For example in a letter of 1868 to John Stanislas Flanagan he went so far as to declare that 'there is nothing which the Church has defined or shall define but what an Apostle, if asked, would have been able fully to answer and would have answered'.[7] That is what leads me to wonder whether, although personal and organic analogies for development are both found, it is the latter that really exercised the more fundamental influence on him, for these entail an essentially teleological continuity in the way that our own often more circuitous patterns of growth do not.[8]

However that may be, it is none the less to the personal that he appeals in explaining how subsequent generations could come to a similar knowledge. It is here that the notion of *phronesis* makes its entry, and in particular Aristotle's stress on the fact that every type of argumentation and reflection must be dependent on its particular type of subject-matter.[9]

[6] E.g. G. O'Collins, 'Newman's Seven Notes: The case of the resurrection' in I. Ker and A. G. Hill (ed.), *Newman After A Hundred Years* (Oxford: Clarendon Press, 1990), pp. 337–52. O'Collins in this instance makes out a plausible case.

[7] Reprinted in J. D. Holmes (ed.), *Theological Papers of John Henry Newman on Biblical Inspiration and on Infallibility* (Oxford: Clarendon Press, 1979), pp. 151–60, esp. 158. For a contemporary endorsement of a similar position, though without reference to Newman: G. Moran, *Theology of Revelation* (London: Search Press, 1973), p. 87.

[8] For a strong argument the other way, W. J. Kelly, 'The doctrine of development: another look at the underlying image' in J. D. Bastable (ed.), *Newman and Gladstone: Centennial Essays* (Dublin: Veritas, 1978), pp. 89–113.

[9] For the extent of his debt to Aristotle's *Nichomachean Ethics* and the absence of a comparable influence from Aristotle's metaphysical works, G. Verbeke, 'Aristotelian roots of Newman's illative sense' in Bastable, pp. 177–95; for a valuable attempt to draw parallels with contemporary philosophy, B. Mitchell, 'Newman as a philosopher' in Ker and Hill, pp. 223–46.

It is not simply a matter of obeying formal logical rules as with more theoretical forms of knowledge but rather of using informal cumulative patterns of reasoning within which a crucial role will have been played by social formation, through the individual having learnt from others and by experience what kind of weight to give to the various factors involved. The importance of such considerations was already quite familiar within the English tradition, even in their application to religious thought, as the pervasive influence of Bishop Butler indicates. The genius of Newman's *Grammar of Assent* thus lies not in an entirely original idea but in grounding more effectively the more widespread relevance of such notions. In the *Grammar*, though, Newman is primarily concerned with very general issues of religious epistemology, especially as these apply to personal decision-making. So it is to a slightly earlier work that we must turn to clarify how he saw such reflections as applying at the corporate level and in particular to the question of doctrinal development. For it is in his essay *On Consulting the Faithful in Matters of Doctrine* that we discover the notion of seeking the *consensus fidelium* conceptualised in terms of 'a sort of instinct, or *phronema*, deep in the mystical bosom of the body of Christ', and glossed, following Mühler, as '*ce sentiment commun, cette conscience de l'Eglise . . . le sens chrétien existant dans l'Eglise . . . fomé de ces vérités et par ces vérités*'.[10]

From a Roman Catholic point of view it is of course important to determine the precise relation between papal declaration and that consensus, and in particular whether the former should ever be seen to substitute for the latter. Could practical wisdom in a community of this sort simply sometimes entail under appropriate circumstances obedience to how one particular inspired mind understands the requirements of *phronesis*? Newman scholars seem divided on whether Newman allowed the possibility of conflict or not.[11] For what it is worth, my own view is that he thought of the two types of approach as necessarily pulling in the same direction, and so the appeal to *phronesis* would actually give independent confirmation of papal decrees. Such optimism, though, seems to me to belie a more complex reality. To illustrate why this is so, I want now to turn to a consideration of the two doctrines I mentioned at the beginning, both in their 1853–4 context and today. What I want to suggest is that,

[10] Coulson edition (London: Collins, 1961), pp. 73–4.

[11] One might contrast Gerard Magill's acceptance of a creative interaction and tension with Thomas Norris' interpretation that the informed conscience will necessarily submit itself to the teaching of the magisterium: G. Magill, 'The living mind: Newman on assent and dissent' in G. Magill (ed.), *Discourse and Context: An Interdisciplinary Study of J. H. Newman* (Carbondale: Southern Illinois University Press, 1993), pp. 144–64; T. J. Norris, *Only Life Gives Life: Revelation, Theology and Christian Living according to Cardinal Newman* (Dublin: Columba, 1996), esp. pp. 139–40.

while Newman was right to identify the key role of more informal considerations in determining the *phronema* of the community, he was wrong
in supposing that such developments are always essentially natural and
obvious. Sharp discontinuities can and do occur, and indeed the whole
process is only fully intelligible long after the decisive change has occurred.
In this at least then, Hegel was right.[12] If hell enables us to see what has
largely already happened in one case, consideration of the immaculate
conception will allow us, surface appearances notwithstanding, to look at
a doctrine still not wholly resolved even for Roman Catholics.

The decline of hell

Certainly, discontinuity seems the most obvious feature of the Church's
changing attitude to hell understood as a place of everlasting punishment.
A virtually unanimous consensus in favour of the doctrine has in little
over a century been transformed into the overwhelming majority on the
other side within Anglicanism and an increasing tendency that way also
within Roman Catholicism. Indicative of this change within Anglicanism
was the recent acceptance by General Synod of a report by the Church of
England Doctrine Commission that explicitly rejected the doctrine,[13] while
within the Roman communion one notes that if the theologian currently
most influential in conservative circles did not actually go so far as to deny
the doctrine, the logic of his discussion is such as virtually to entail that
hell must be empty. A fascinating illustration of the latter is the contrasting
treatments given by Balthasar to Charles Péguy's doubts on the one hand
(favourably endorsed) and on the other to Dante's depiction of hell (its
very intelligibility is questioned).[14] Nor was Newman himself entirely
immune from this process. For, if some of his remarks on the topic sound
like orthodox endorsement of the belief,[15] there are others that read
suspiciously like deliberate attempts to weaken its impact. Thus one finds
him as a Roman Catholic both insisting that 'eternal' does not mean endless
succession and that, even if it did, it would be doubtful if hell would be
experienced as such since 'intense pain destroys the recognition of time, or
a succession of minutes and hours'.[16] Not dissimilar arguments are in fact

---

[12] Taking perhaps his famous remark as entailing full intelligibility only in retrospect: 'the
owl of Minerva begins its flight only with the fall of dusk' (*Philosophy of Right*, Preface).

[13] *The Mystery of Salvation* (London: Church House, 1995), pp. 198–9.

[14] Both discussions are to be found in *The Glory of the Lord*, III (Edinburgh: T&T Clark,
1986). Because justice is the sole criterion, we are told that 'nothing can happen in Dante's
hell . . . since love is the interior motive force of all things' (p. 90).

[15] For an example, *Discourses to Mixed Congregations* (1881), pp. 38–9.

[16] For this and other relevant quotations, G. Rowell, *Hell and the Victorians* (Oxford:
Clarendon Press, 1974), esp. pp. 142, 161.

found in Maurice, who, as well as appealing to biblical assertions that God is love and wills all to be saved, also insists that 'eternal' indicates a particular quality of life rather than endless succession.[17]

On such a basis a natural temptation might be to suggest one single key factor for change, a different understanding of the meaning of Scripture. It is one of the great strengths of Newman's general analysis that he warns against any such simple hypothesis. Of course, some passages did come to be read in a new way, and indeed biblical scholars helped with the process as the source for the image of Gehenna became clearer, as also the way in which Matthew considerably expands what occurs only minimally in Mark.[18] Even so, however much theologians such as Barth and Balthasar might want to assert that it is simply the pressure of the text alone that forces the new reading, there seems little doubt that something more complicated is in fact going on. After all, for almost two millennia the Church had insisted on keeping the love and judgement of Christ together in tension and in so doing had ensured a maximising reading of Scripture, with no passage forced into subordination to any other and, whatever might be said of the rest of the New Testament, it remains true that Matthew and the Book of Revelation seem to point decisively in a quite different direction with hell firmly endorsed. A non-infallibilist view of Scripture could of course claim that rejection was on balance the import of the biblical witness, but, however much this may eventually have been the line taken subsequently by theologians and their churches, it is implausible as an interpretation of what was occurring at the roots of the change in the nineteenth century. For at this stage the great mass of Christians still held to a stricter view of biblical authority, agonise though they might over the doctrine of hell. Other factors must therefore be sought.

The first concerns changing attitudes to human responsibility and punishment. It is perhaps worth drawing attention to three aspects of this. The first is changing attitudes to infinities. Intellectual historians have pointed out the way in which in the nineteenth century the growth of limited liability in law was also reflected in changing conceptions of the atonement,[19] but to see the full extent of the difference one might go further back in history and contrast Anselm's views with what comes later. For a key element in Anselm's argument in *Cur Deus Homo* is that simply in

---

[17] F. D. Maurice, *Theological Essays* (London: James Clarke, 1957), 'Concluding essay', esp. pp. 305–6, 314.

[18] Matthew has 'weeping and gnashing of teeth' six times, 'outer darkness' three times. On the only Marcan occurrence of such language; cf. e.g. D. E. Nineham, *Saint Mark* (Harmondsworth: Penguin, 1961), p. 125.

[19] B. Hilton, *The Age of the Atonement* (Oxford: Clarendon Press, 1988), esp. pp. 255–97. One example he quotes is F. W. Farrar's *Eternal Hope* of 1878, itself influenced by Maurice.

virtue of being born we already owe God an infinite obligation and so nothing that we can do can recompense him for any wrong we may have done. The other side of that argument is of course that in virtue of God being our creator he can do with us as he will, and versions of this claim are indeed to be found deeply embedded throughout the Christian tradition, in writers as varied as Paul and Aquinas.[20] Yet just as the once common belief that parents possess similar rights has given place to the conviction that any such work of creation or power must bring with it reciprocal responsibilities, so too has a similar thing happened in the divine case. It is often said that it is the horrors of the Holocaust that have generated the preoccupation with theodicy in modern theology, but in my view no less important is this conviction that even an all-powerful creator cannot be morally divorced from mutual responsibilities. Then, secondly, one notes the growth in stress on subjective responsibility rather than objectively wrong action and its consequences. So, if in earlier systems of punishment it was thought sufficient to identify who had done the deed, one notes from Abelard onwards an increased emphasis on locating the precise intention with which the deed was done (which might lessen or increase culpability). If this process was aided in the medieval period by reflection on sacramental confession and the appropriate penances to be applied, it has also been further advanced in our own day by insights such as Freud's into the complexities of human motivation. In other words, the absolute character of evil was effectively being undermined through such changes, and so the appropriateness of infinite punishment made more questionable. Then, finally, there was the emergence of different attitudes to retribution. If many continue to have a gut feeling in favour of such a response to the more heinous of crimes, there are also strong counter-currents that suggest that the only charitable response is one which insists that retribution only makes sense in so far as it provides the means to effect a change in the person's character, whether through forcing them into a recognition that they have done wrong or else in enabling training that could lead to reform. Inevitably, such a perspective on the human case has also once more had its impact on how any divine action might be understood.

The way in which I have expressed this group of considerations could be read in purely secular terms, and for some that will be enough to provide grounds for rejection, whereas others might find in them the out-workings of a natural theology. Yet others might wish each to be rephrased in purely biblical or explicitly Christian language, and only when that is done would

---

[20] For Paul, cf. Romans 9:20ff. Aquinas asserts in various places that God has the right to abrogate laws against murder, theft and adultery because everything that is belongs to him as its creator.

they then be seen to be acceptable. Again, though, I would wish to resist any such tidying operation, and for two reasons, the one historical and the other conceptual. On the historical front, the problem is that it seems implausible to claim that in so far as such attitudes have emerged within Christianity they have been entirely self-generated. As my examples of sacramental confession and Freud were meant to show, Christianity has also been in dialogue with the wider culture in which it is set, sometimes contributing and sometimes receiving. Again, if we turn to the truth as distinct from the history of such considerations, there is equally no reason why we must put things in terms of stark alternatives. If one believes in natural theology as I do, then along with Grotius one might well believe that such considerations could be expressed for the benefit of the non-believer, *etsi non Deus daretur* ('as if God did not exist'). Equally though, they can be given an explicitly religious hue, not least by appealing to the kind of value God assigns to each human being in the life of Christ as God incarnate. But what remains dangerous is if this is insisted upon as a way of avoiding outside debts, for that way the Church simply disguises from itself how much more widely God works than within its own particular treasures, whether these be Scripture or its wider tradition. Newman is so convinced of the divine character of the Church that it is, I think, a danger to which he himself succumbs; Maurice might have provided a useful corrective.[21]

The final range of factors which I want to mention are imaginative. These one might expect to have been of particular interest to Newman, not least because it looks as though his key distinction between notional and real assent was in fact originally made in terms of the notional and the imaginative.[22] But, if that suggests a positive estimate of the imagination's role, more negative references need also to be noted. Indeed, in response to one objector to hell he observes that 'in spite of the word of Scripture, your imagination would carry you away', while elsewhere he cautions: 'Imagination is distinct from reason, but mistaken for it. What is strange, is to the imagination false'.[23] In that nuanced approach of recognising both imagination's strengths and its limitations, I believe him in general to have been right, but in this particular instance to have drawn the wrong conclusions, as also on the immaculate conception. For, in effect, Newman allows dogma always to override the questions posed by the imagination rather than conceding that sometimes at least they might be right.

[21] Helpfully argued in J. Coulson, *Newman and the Common Tradition* (Oxford: Clarendon Press, 1970), esp. pp. 187–205.

[22] So J. Coulson in *Religion and Imagination* (Oxford: Clarendon Press, 1981), pp. 60, 82–3.

[23] J. D. Holmes (ed.), *The Theological Papers of John Henry Newman on Faith and Certainty* (Oxford: Clarendon Press, 1976), pp. 147, 47.

Elsewhere I have traced how images of hell were applied across the centuries, and suggested that they move from a biblical pattern where they are applied essentially to those outside the community to one where increasingly they are used as instruments for encouraging self-judgement, as in the inclusion in depictions of contemporaries and clergy.[24] My aim in so doing was to try to understand the reasons for the elements in the biblical picture against which so many of us now revolt (a small community resentful of its treatment by its stronger and larger neighbours) and also why in the providence of God such a pattern should have persisted so long (it was in fact transformed into a more profound use, in encouraging self-judgement).[25] Here, however, we need to ask the question why the image has now collapsed altogether. So far as the Reformation is concerned, it is worth noting that its effect was to externalise the image once more. For Reformation insistence that faith brought with it internal assurance of salvation meant that hell could only be applied to others, and so, if initially that brought a reinforcement of the biblical pattern (with Roman Catholics now substituting for Romans and Jews), in the long term it was to lead to the image's demise, as more pluralistic societies forced recognition of the value inhering in those with whom one disagreed. Roman Catholics of course turned the belief outwards as well, but what made this more acceptable was that the same belief was also directed inwards in images aimed at rigorous self-questioning. Some of the exercises proposed by St Alphonsus Liguori in the eighteenth century and still being practised in the nineteenth are a case in point.[26] But in the end these too failed, and ironically the failure can already be seen in Newman. For, although as we have noted he sometimes resorted to the imagery of hell, his most lasting influence on concepts of the after-life was to come with his *Dream of Gerontius* of 1865. Significantly, in that work any sense of purgatory as a place of punishment, a lesser hell as it were, disappears and in its place comes God purging the soul of its imperfections in what might be described as a bitter-sweet experience. The wider lesson being learnt by society as a whole was now applied here also: progress and education best proceed through encouragement rather than through deprivation and punishment.

Although what I have identified above seem to me historically the most important factors that lead to the change, it is important that neither the way in which they exercised their impact nor their legitimacy as arguments should be misunderstood. It is, I suspect, very much easier for us at the

[24] D. Brown, *Discipleship and Imagination* (Oxford: Oxford University Press, 2000), pp. 127–62.

[25] For an accessible example of the technique in action; cf. Anselm's Second Meditation in *Prayers and Meditations* (London: Penguin, 1973), pp. 225–9, esp. 227–8.

[26] For some examples, Rowell, pp. 154–7.

beginning of the twenty-first century to understand what has happened than it would have been for those engaged in the process at the time. Arguments and considerations can often be in the air without ever being adequately conceptualised, and where the influences on the Church are external it may indeed be dangerous or counterproductive to make these explicit. It is vital, therefore, not to confuse how matters were discussed at the time with what can be seen in retrospect as the total range of relevant considerations. Ironically, therefore, bringing all such factors now to the surface may well provide a stronger retrospective cumulative argument for change than was thought to be available at the time.

The immaculate conception

In the case of the immaculate conception (the doctrine that Mary was from the very moment of her conception exempt from original sin), the issues are, I think, quite different. Here we have Newman's adopted communion moving in one particular direction, and the rest of Christendom resisting. Indeed, there is some evidence to suggest that, whereas in the previous two centuries Orthodoxy had showed some similar tendencies that way, it now united in opposition.[27] A century and more on, and it is possible to detect competing pressures even within Roman Catholicism itself that bear on how the dogma should be understood. Space requires that I focus my discussion on some limited aspect; so what I would like to do is illustrate the relevance of Newman's notion of the *phronimos*, and in particular how practical wisdom is needed in ensuring that apparently legitimate arguments are not carried to their full logical conclusion. If in the patristic period acute sensitivity was vital in ensuring that Alexandrian stress on Christ's divinity and Antiochene on his humanity were not allowed to undermine the Church's claim that Jesus was both fully God and fully man, so on this issue constant vigilance is necessary to avoid one step too far creating a quite different Christian reality. I shall illustrate the point by noting three types of argument (biblical, analogical, and imaginative) and the inherent dangers they contain, should they be carried to their seemingly legitimate conclusion.

To some it may seem extraordinary that mention should even be made in this context of Scripture, but, as Pusey concedes in his *Eirenicon*, God's providential fore-ordaining of events is in fact the common biblical pattern, and in at least two other cases (Jeremiah and John the Baptist) that

---

[27] So K. Ware, 'The Mother of God in Orthodox theology and devotion' in A. Stacpoole (ed.), *Mary's Place in Christian Dialogue* (Slough: St Paul Publications, 1982), pp. 169–81, esp. 176.

predestining also begins before birth.[28] In Mary's case there is of course no explicit statement to this effect, but at least in pushing the decisive intervention of God further back in the story it is clear that there is a defensible and thoroughly biblical aim, to stress the priority of divine grace throughout, in enabling Mary to fulfil her role. That is no doubt why there had long been a consensus not only that Mary was sinless but also that grace had been operating in her right from her presence in her mother's womb. Proverbs 8, 22ff. was taken as indicative of the eternal divine plan, and so to exempt her from original sin might seem but a small, further implication to draw from this larger scheme.[29]

But one would be wrong. Original sin as such will concern us in a moment. There is, however, a more basic issue to be faced first, and that is how grace operates. Barth objected to the dogma that it undermined an essential biblical principle, that of *sola gratia*, but ironically, it seems to me that, if anything, it does the reverse, and enhances it. For, if accepted, it would mean that Mary's fiat to the angel is seen as only possible because of preordaining grace. That is why Balthasar's exposition of the significance of Mary can in many ways be seen as a natural development of Barth's earlier emphases. For if Barth speaks of Mary in the annunciation as a model of 'non-willing, non-achieving, non-creative, non-sovereign man . . . who can merely receive',[30] so for Balthasar she becomes the pattern of the Church as feminine, obedient receiving.[31] But are either Barth or Balthasar right? Certainly, elsewhere the New Testament very much stresses personal initiative and responsibility and so a more active form of discipleship. It could therefore be argued that this is the inference to draw from the Bible as a whole which could then be turned back on the annunciation passage, to limit its impact in terms of anticipated passivity, whether at the hands of God or otherwise. We find Newman resistant to talk of Mary as mere 'instrument';[32] yet, if all the emphasis is on the divine initiative, and on Mary as uniquely endowed to make her choice, it is hard to see how else she is to be described. Are those who respond positively with less divine help not to be more admired, if only because they are more like us? Putting it another way, if

[28] E. B. Pusey, *Eirenikon* (1869), e.g. II, pp. 52 and 392.

[29] The passage was first taken to refer to Christ, but as Wisdom is female and the tradition had already grown up of alluding to Mary as the seat of Wisdom (Christ as Wisdom sits on her lap), the further move was perhaps inevitable.

[30] K. Barth, *Church Dogmatics* I/2 (Edinburgh: T&T Clark, 1958), p. 191. Cf. also p. 194.

[31] To which a male priesthood is necessarily contrasted as *in persona Christi*, and so as receiving from the Father but also giving to the Church at large. For a critique, see my *Discipleship and Imagination*, pp. 274–8.

[32] *Difficulties* (1891), II, p. 41.

80

Mary's 'free choice' is now to be made in conditions essentially different from our own, without any of the more corrupting human pressures towards resistance, that inevitably makes her correspondingly less relevant to how we act.

Newman, though, believes that he has a stronger argument than direct appeal to Scripture, and that is what we might call the analogical argument, the inference from the parallel with Eve: that if Eve was exempt from original sin, so too must Mary be.[33] Underlying the argument is the conviction that in the providence of God he would do all things fair and well, and so one should expect a harmony or proportion in all he does.[34] So, if Christ is the New Adam, it is legitimate to expect Mary to function as the New Eve. The most obvious difficulty with such an appeal is that since Darwin there remain few grounds for believing in a specific historical figure called Eve or even necessarily one first, innocent pair. Almost certainly the earliest version of *homo sapiens* would have had the same tendencies towards sin as ourselves. Of course, even with that acknowledged, one could still try to find in Adam and Eve the human ideal, but it is the proposed parallel as such that creates the problems, not just one specific expression. Thus, for example, the Genesis story presupposes that human perfection should entail the absence both of death and of pain in childbirth. The latter belief developed early, while in respect of the former even as late as 1950 in the formulation of the dogma of the Assumption care was taken to allow just such a possibility for Mary.[35] But was not Newman wiser, if more inconsistent, in resisting such a conclusion, because it would remove Mary not only further from us but also from dependence on her Son?[36] Therein, of course, lies the main objection, that even if the dogma explicitly asserts that Mary pre-emptively at her conception enjoyed the benefits of her Son's work on earth,[37] in practice it now becomes all too easy to separate the two. As Pusey observes, however much that may always have been the Church's official teaching, in actual practice there had long been an increasing tendency to allow Mary to act

[33] Ibid., pp. 31–61.

[34] Commonly summarised in the adage: '*potuit, decuit, fecit*' (it was possible, it was fitting, therefore it was done).

[35] An early allusion to a painless birth is in the *Odes of Solomon* XIX. Pius XII allowed an ambiguous phrase that need not imply physical death: *post terrestrem hanc vitam*. For a helpful analysis and critique, J. McHugh, 'The doctrine of the Immaculate Conception' in A. Stacpoole (ed.), *Mary in Doctrine and Devotion* (Dublin: Columba Press, 1990), pp. 23–33.

[36] *Difficulties* II, pp. 48–9, 125–7. Newman's stress, though, is on her being included ' in Adam's sentence' (p. 48).

[37] The decree used the following phraseology: *Intuitu meritorum Christi Iesu Salvatoris humani generis.*

81

independently of her Son, something he has no difficulty in amply demonstrating in numerous quotations from saints and theologians across the centuries.[38] Its most common form was the portrayal of Mary as the source of mercy in contrast to her judgmental Son. A little step too far had in fact resulted in a considerable distortion of the Christian gospel. Present pressure towards declaring Mary co-redemptrix might be seen as attempting to bring the work of Mary and Christ once more closer together, but what Protestants fear is that, so far from correcting this trend, such an honorific title will merely accentuate the sense of her being fundamentally different from the rest of us.[39]

Finally, there are the imaginative arguments. There is little doubt about the extent to which political factors lay behind the change of iconography that takes place from the seventeenth century onwards,[40] nor about the way in which political conclusions were explicitly or implicitly drawn from the series of visions that were inspired by this new form of imagery.[41] Thanks to a particular reading of Revelation 12, Mary now appeared alone and in triumph over not just the world but also the moon and the stars, and even hell itself.[42] Sometimes, as in Velasquez's famous painting, the suggestion is the acceptable one of the triumph of young innocence, and it is of course important to celebrate Mary as a human being in her own right, both in her growth to adulthood and in reaction to her Son, but it cannot be denied that such legitimate concerns have also sometimes brought with them more sinister implications. Roman Catholic writers are sometimes

[38] Although there is a brief reference in that part of the *Eirenikon* addressed to Newman (1870, III, pp. 331–3), the most damning quotations are to be found in his letter to Keble: ibid. (1865), I, pp. 115–89.

[39] One recent work defends the title on the grounds that 'her status as Co-Redeemer mirrors our own invitation to be co-redeemers': G. D'Costa, *Sexing the Trinity* (London: SCM Press, 2000), esp. pp. 30–5. While such a reading might well be widely acceptable outside Roman Catholic circles, the problem remains that the title also opens up the possibility of more divisive interpretations such as those of Leonardo Boff, where Mary is in effect divinised: *The Maternal Face of God* (London: Collins, 1989), e.g. p. 93.

[40] For her use in bolstering the Spanish monarchy, see my *Discipleship and Imagination*, pp. 265–6; for the effects of a bad christology mentioned later in the paragraph, pp. 250–60.

[41] The message and use of Fatima is perhaps the most obvious case in point: M. Warner, *Alone Of All Her Sex* (London: Quartet, 1978), pp. 313–14.

[42] If the claim of the eighteenth-century Belgian Dominican, John Ketwigh, that Mary 'can mercifully free men certain of their damnation, and who have already died in the state of damnation' is well beyond what most would be prepared to claim, the image of Mary obtaining some remission of the pains of hell was a popular one. For former, see H. Graef, *Mary: A History of Doctrine and Devotion* (London: Sheed & Ward, 1965), II, p. 69; for the latter and the eighth- or ninth-century story of Mary's visit to hell, P. Pascal, *The Religion of the Russian People* (London: Mowbrays, 1976), pp. 57–81.

themselves found worrying about Mary being so wholly dissociated from her Son and from others,[43] but one might add it is part of a long-standing phenomenon whereby Mary came to function in her own right, even in saving from Hell.[44] It would be a travesty of the complexities of history to suggest even for a moment that talk of the immaculate conception of Mary of itself generated this distortion, but equally it would be hard to deny that it did act as a reinforcement. As I have argued elsewhere, a distorted image of a stern, judgmental Christ gave added pressure for a more august but still gentle Mary to play the substitute role, and in those terms one can easily understand why the immaculate conception could be seen as the culmination of a long but perverted process of development. Fortunately, that image of Christ along with the associated image of hell is fading, and so with it the need for Mary as the kind of independent figure of power of which much of her treatment as immaculately conceived has been a part.

One further imaginative problem remains to be noted, and that is the virtual impossibility of separating the doctrine from notions of sexual intercourse as inherently sinful. For, even if it is maintained that the doctrine does not necessarily commit one to an Augustinian understanding of how original sin is transmitted, the very combination of those two words, 'conception' and 'immaculate', make it hard not to suppose that normal conception is seen as necessarily 'stained'. If anyone doubts such an effect in today's climate, they need only recall the pop star Madonna's choice of name and the type of themes of which she sings, not least in her album, *The Immaculate Collection* (1990).

In each case, then, what we have in my view is relevant considerations carried too far: a rightful stress on the indispensability of divine grace transformed into an exclusivity that reduces the human contribution to something purely passive; a reversal of the myth of the Fall transformed into a one–one correspondence that excludes Mary from pain in pregnancy and from death; due recognition that the significance of Mary's life is not simply reducible to that of her Son transformed into her acting independently of him. Some Roman Catholics are aware of these dangers, and it may be that one day the doctrine will be expressed in a form generally acceptable to Christians at large. Certainly, the twentieth century witnessed both an advance and then a retreat from the notion of Mary as

---

[43] So S. J. Boss, *Empress and Handmaid* (London: Cassell, 2000), pp. 140–6, where she argues that the earlier imagery of Anne and Joachim at the Golden Gate was healthier.

[44] Newman himself uses Revelation 12 with its imagery of the defeat of the dragon/serpent/Devil to question: 'what height of glory may we not attribute to her?': *Difficulties* II, pp. 57–61.

co-redemptrix.[45] It could even be that one day the dogma retreats from Catholic horizons in much the same way as another papal pronouncement which Newman defended, the Syllabus of Errors, has already retreated into the mists of history.[46] On the other hand, as in 1854, the Roman Catholic church may once more come to see itself as required to act 'contra mundum'.

Conclusion

None of us can predict the future. What, though, I can hazard is some final thoughts on where Newman's various analyses now stand more than a century later. While he was right about the centrality of issues of development, on the negative side it seems that he exhibited a confidence about the smoothness of their course to which, if my account of changing attitudes to hell is correct, we are no longer entitled. Even a virtually universal consensus across denominations and across the centuries is no infallible guide. Again, he was right about the need for *phronesis* in considering theological arguments and their limitations; the sadness was that he failed to see that this applied no less to some aspects of Christianity he was called on to defend in his own day. He failed to take seriously Pusey's complaints about the direction in which much current Catholic piety was going, and equally could only offer specious explanations of why no weight should be attached to the views of those fathers who questioned even the sinlessness of Mary.[47] Ironically, one of his greatest virtues was inconsistency (intense pain by its very nature cannot be everlasting; Mary did die), for this shows that he too was after all listening. For it is surely by listening to one another that the *phronema* of the Christian community as a whole may one day be shaped to a common mind. If with Mary many of the issues remain unresolved, how much change is possible is well illustrated by the huge transformation in attitudes to hell that has occurred since 1853. If to say this much is to reject any simple notion of the infallibility or even the indefectibility of the Church, it is not to deny the reality of the Church's growth into the truth, however convoluted that process may be. It was the genius of Newman to alert us to the complexity of theological argument, and that

---

[45] A good example of the sea-change in much Roman Catholic thinking is the contrast between Edward Schillebeeckx's later views and those expressed in his earlier *Mary, Mother of the Redemption* (London: Sheed & Ward, London, 1964), where not only is the notion of co-redemptrix defended (e.g. pp. 126–30) but inflated language used throughout (e.g. p. 67 – Christ on the cross 'suffered first and foremost and most of all for Mary').

[46] The larger part of *Difficulties* II is in fact taken up with a response to Gladstone's objections to the Syllabus: pp. 171–378.

[47] For the former, note his own use of extravagant language, *Difficulties* II, pp. 37, 62, 78, 80; for the latter, ibid., pp. 135–6, 140–3.

complexity needs practical wisdom on the part of us all if the various and often conflicting considerations are to be appropriately balanced.

One last thought. I am conscious that throughout I have been dealing with the rejection of doctrines rather than their elaboration. That was in part determined by which issues came to prominence in Newman's own day. Even so, I should end by noting the positive side of these two questions. The obverse side of hell is of course how we conceive of the love of God, while the obverse of the immaculate conception is what it is to be one of Christ's saints. It is precisely because I regard Mary as the pre-eminent model for faith that I want her firmly one of us and equally firmly clearly dependent on her Son. That way Mary as victor over hell may disappear, but in its place comes Mary the loving and suffering mother welcomed by her Son to reign with him in heaven.[48]

[48] I am grateful to Robert Hannaford, Ann Loades, Basil Mitchell and Geoffrey Rowell for comments on an earlier draft of this paper.

Newman and Manning: The Ecclesiological Issues

JAMES PEREIRO

The publication by the Vatican Congregation for the Doctrine of the Faith of the declaration *Dominus Jesus* (August 2000) raised at the time a storm of comments in the general press and in specialised publications. Although the declaration was concerned mainly with the unicity and universality of the salvific mystery of Jesus Christ, the attention of commentators was focused on its treatment of the unicity and unity of the Church, comprising sections 16 and 17 out of a total of 23. Criticism was directed mainly against the criteria used to distinguish between Churches and Ecclesial Communities, and, in particular, on the fact that the Declaration seemed to include among the latter Anglicans and Lutheran Protestants.

These reactions served as a reminder that ecumenical dialogue on ecclesiological matters involves several processes of reflection. It demands firstly the generating of a self-awareness about what constitutes a Church and how that concept is incarnated in the respective community. It also entails a process of recognition of the partner's self-awareness, together with a perception of one's ecclesiological status in the other's eyes. It is in this line that a recent document of the House of Bishops of the Church of England acknowledges that the term 'Catholic' is understood in different senses by Anglicans and Catholics.[1]

The present paper tries to explore how Newman and Manning, during their Anglican years, dealt with ecclesiological concepts – communion, unity, universal Church, particular Church, etc. – involved in the afore-mentioned processes of self-awareness and recognition. It then goes on to

[1] *The Eucharist: Sacrament of Unity*. An Occasional Paper of the House of Bishops of the Church of England (London: Church Publishing House, 2001), nn. 34 *et al.*

compare their treatment with present official Catholic teaching on those matters.

1. Newman and Manning: an ecclesiology of communion

The ecclesiology of the Oxford Movement can be called in all property a theology of the mystical body of Christ or of the Communion of Saints. Härdelin, however, pointed out that 'the idea of the Church as an organism, as the mystical body of Christ, which forms so prominent a feature of the thought of the Fathers, was not developed by the Tractarians until a later stage'.[2] Even then, in Härdelin's appreciation, no Tractarian – with the exception perhaps of Robert Wilberforce – 'ever worked out a systematic and thorough ecclesiology, not to speak of an entire theological system'.[3] This may be open to question, especially if we consider Henry Edward Manning as belonging to the fringe of the Tractarian Movement. For he developed a rich and highly articulate ecclesiological synthesis towards the end of his Anglican life. It is an interesting fact that, while Newman's materials for a theology of the Church are dispersed through his sermons and other works, Manning's ecclesiological concerns found expression in a few dense works, particularly his *The Unity of the Church* (1842) and his fourth volume of *Sermons* (1850).

Manning's original insight into the role of the Holy Spirit within the Church, which can be dated around the months March–April 1847, led him to perceive the richness of the notion of the Church as the mystical body of Christ. That vision which, for him, had almost the character of a particular revelation, was to be the guiding light of all his subsequent theological development. At the heart of the mystery of the Church Manning found the mystery of the Incarnation. The communion with God, to which humanity had been called *ab initio*, is now to be achieved by our partaking of the manhood of the incarnate Word: man is divinised by his contact with the divine through union with Christ's human nature.[4] This is no nominal union, nor is it an accidental one, like the coming together of minds which agree in certain opinions and gather under the umbrella of a collective name (Aristotelians, Platonists, and the like). The union of the mystical body is a 'substantial' union, in Manning's phrase, like that of

[2] A. Härdelin, *The Tractarian Understanding of the Eucharist* (Uppsala: University Press, 1965), p. 72; see Newman's synthetic description of the mystical body of Christ in the sermon 'The Unity of the Church', *Parochial and Plain Sermons [PPS]*, vii, 17 (London, 1899), pp. 231–3.

[3] A. Härdelin, *Tractarian Understanding*, p. 84.

[4] Cf. H. E. Manning, *Sermons (ASer)*, iv, 10 (London, 1850), pp. 181ff.

the parts of a living whole.[5] This is the work of the Holy Spirit: the agent of the union of the divine and the human natures in Christ is also the agent of man's union with Christ, making us one in Him who had died and is alive. Before the coming of the Holy Spirit, those who had followed Christ were connected by discipleship rather than by an inward principle; after his coming they are all organs of an invisible body, animated by the same life, governed by one soul and one directing mind, a real living body, Newman would say, not a mere framework artificially arranged to look like one.[6]

At the root and centre of the mystical body of Christ is found the sacramental system, the source of its unity and life. First of all, baptism, by means of which the Christian is incorporated into the mystical body of Christ, becoming entitled to the gift of the Holy Spirit[7] and engrafted into the stock of the Word made flesh.[8] If the natural body of Christ is the stock onto which the Christian is engrafted through baptism, the sacramental presence of his Body and Blood sustains the life of the individual members and of the Church.[9] Manning would conclude: 'The natural body of our Lord Jesus Christ is, as it were, the root out of which, by the power of the Holy Ghost, His mystical body is produced.'[10]

This mystical body, therefore, is not the result of the coming together of individual Christians: it pre-existed them. Each Christian has been made such by being taken into the body through baptism, and in this way 'individuals are incorporated into an already existing body'. As Newman put it, if everyone 'who wishes to become a Christian must come to an existing visible body for the gift [of Baptism] (. . .) it is plain that no number of men can ever, consistently with Christ's intention, set up a Church for themselves'.[11] The Church has been constituted by Christ as the public body of Christians, regulated by certain rules and governed by its proper offices, and in it are to be found the means of grace and of instruction.[12]

Newman and Manning took special care to defend the visible nature of the Church and its unity. The former, when dealing with the visible unity

[5] Cf. ibid., p. 187; J. H. Newman, *PPS*, iv, 11 (London, 1900), pp. 169–70.
[6] Cf. J. H. Newman, *PPS*, iv, 11, pp. 169–71; see also H. E. Manning, *ASer*, iv, pp. 89, 103 and 187.
[6] Cf. J. H. Newman, MS 118, p. 12, 20 November 1825, quoted in J. Tolhurst, *The Church . . . a Communion – in the preaching of John Henry Newman* (Leominster: Fowler Wright Books, 1988), p. 30; see also H. E. Manning, *ASer*, iv, 11, p. 201.
[8] Cf. J. H. Newman, *PPS*, vii, 17, p. 235; see also H. E. Manning, *ASer*, iv, 11, pp. 198–9.
[9] Cf. H.E. Manning, *ASer*, iv, 11, p. 198.
[10] Ibid.
[11] J. H. Newman, *PPS*, vii, 17, p. 235.
[12] Cf. J. H. Newman, MS 162, pp. 4–5, quoted in J. Tolhurst, *The Church*, pp. 38–9.

of the Church, saw it emerging from the general drift of the whole divine plan and from the particular will of Christ, who prayed that believers might be one in affection and action: 'what possible way is there', he exclaimed, 'of many men acting *together*, except that of forming themselves into a visible body or society, regulated by certain laws and officers? and how can they act on a large scale, and consistently, unless it be a permanent body?'[13] When confronted with the reality of the particular Church, Newman saw it as the realisation in time and space of the universal Church, and he made use of an analogy to describe the relationship between them: 'as the soul of man is in every part of his body; (. . .) not so in any one part, head or heart, hands or feet, as not to be in every other; so also the heavenly Jerusalem, the mother of our new birth is in all lands at once, fully and entirely as a spirit'.[14] The particular Church – bishop and pastors, together with the faithful depending on them – is on those bases '*called* the Church, though really but a fragment of it, as being that part of it which is seen and can be pointed out, and as resembling it in type, and witnessing it, and leading towards it'.[15] Newman added here an important qualification: baptism does not admit the person receiving it into the particular but into the universal Church, through the porch, as it were, of the English, Greek or Roman Churches.[16]

Manning shared those ideas, and later made them explicit in his campaign against the Gorham judgement. 'The Church in every land,' he wrote, 'is the Church throughout the world sojourning as in a place, and there teaching and ruling by the whole weight of the Divine Office committed to the Church Universal.'[17] The local or particular Church has no life except in so far as it is part of the Church Universal and in so far as the latter is present and active in it: 'every particular Church speaks to the local Sovereignty with the voice and authority of the universal Church'.[18]

For both, Newman and Manning, the local bishop played a vital role in the being and action of the particular Church. They often quoted the doctrine of St Ignatius of Antioch about the place of the bishop as chief representative of Christ, source of authority, channel of grace and ultimate centre of unity, deliberation and discipline in the diocese; no power, except the collective authority of the whole Episcopal order, Manning said, can

[13] J. H. Newman, *PPS*, vii, 17, p. 235.
[14] J. H. Newman, *PPS*, iv, 11, p. 175.
[15] Ibid., p. 174.
[16] Cf. ibid., p. 176.
[17] H. E. Manning, *The Appellate Jurisdiction of the Crown in Matters Spiritual. A Letter to the Right Reverend Ashurst-Turner, Lord Bishop of Chichester* (London, 1850), p. 22.
[18] Ibid., p. 21.

reach the faithful unless it reaches them with the bishop's express permission.[19] This was perhaps the first notion they gained from their study of the Fathers: 'a vivid perception of the divine institution, and the prerogatives, and the gifts of the Episcopate'.[20] The unity and life of the particular or local church is ensured by the bishop, through the exercise of the power granted him by Apostolic Succession: through it the powers entrusted by Christ to the Apostles descend to his ministers today. A break in that succession would imply the end of that particular line of witness, authority and powers: 'what man [would] dare, on his own authority, renew what the authority of Christ began?'[21] Newman, in similar vein, would add: 'if men cannot administer to themselves the rite of regeneration, it is surely as little or much less reasonable to suppose that they could become bishops or priests on their own ordination'.[22]

Particular Churches do not need to be united together for their completeness, 'except by the tie of descent from one original [Church]', and Apostolic Succession is sufficient title to claim that descent. Newman, in accord with Anglican tradition, thought at first that mutual intercourse was an accident of the Church, and not of its essence: each diocese is a perfect independent Church, sufficient for itself; and the unity of the Church consists not in a mutual understanding, intercourse and combination among Christians or in what they do in common, but in what they are and have in common, in their possession of the succession, their Episcopal form, their Apostolic faith, and the use of the sacraments.[23] Newman added, however, that although the Episcopate was sufficient for the being or essence of a particular Church, for its well being or health 'it should be united with bonds of active intercourse with all its branches'.[24] Church cannot stand aloof from Church without sin, and separation works to the detriment of all parties.[25] Within this general theory, schism is not perceived as estrangement of Church from Church but as a breaking of the structure of the local church by separating from the bishop or setting up altar against altar.[26]

---

[19] Cf. H. E. Manning, *The Principle of the Ecclesiastical Commission Examined, in a Letter to The Right Revd Lord Bishop of Chichester* (London, 1838), pp. 5–6; see also H. E. Manning, *The English Church: Its Succession and Witness for Christ* (London, 1835), pp. 9–10; also J. H. Newman, 'The Catholicity of the Anglican Church', *British Critic* (January, 1840) in *Essays Critical and Historical*, ii (London, 1897), p. 32.

[20] J. H. Newman, *Certain Difficulties felt by Anglicans in Catholic Teaching*, i (London, 1897), pp. 371–2.

[21] H. E. Manning, *English Church*, p. 9.

[22] J. H. Newman, *PPS*, vii, 17, p. 238.

[23] J. H. Newman, 'Catholicity of the Anglican Church', pp. 18 and 20.

[24] Ibid., p. 38.

[25] Cf. ibid., p. 33.

[26] Cf. ibid., pp. 23 and 30.

v

Manning, for his part, discussed what constitutes Church unity in his book *The Unity of the Church*. That the Church was one, he said, was not under discussion: all Christians confess that article of the Creed. The question posed by the divisions among Christians was *how* the Church is one. Manning approached the subject by distinguishing between an organic or objective unity and a subjective or moral one. He defined the first as 'the identity of the Church of any age with the church of the Apostles in the faith and sacraments, and in the commission received from Christ, and transmitted by lawful succession'.[27] The subjective unity of the Church, on the other hand, consists in unity of communion at two levels: first, submission to the lawful pastor of the local church; secondly, charity in relationships with the several Churches dispersed throughout the world. Organic unity was the guarantee of the 'personal identity' of the present Church with the Church of the Apostles;[28] while subjective unity – at the level of communion among local churches – might be broken without destroying the unity of the Church. In breaking the latter, Anglicans, Greeks or Romans, in spite of their separation from each other, had not broken the unity of the Church or separated from the communion with the one Head of the Church in heaven.[29] This did not mean that they had not suffered because of their divisions; the loss of the *sacramentum unitatis* had given rise to corruptions in doctrine and discipline, although these had not amounted to formal heresy. Since the breach between the branches of the Church, Newman could say, 'Truth has not dwelt simply and securely in any visible Tabernacle'.[30] It was precisely because of those corruptions that the Church of England had separated from Rome, in an effort to restore and preserve the purity of primitive Christianity.

Both Manning and Newman originally accepted the Branch Theory of the unity of the Church. This claimed that the Church's original perfect peace and unity all over the world had been subsequently shattered by divisions and quarrels. As a result, that 'vast Catholic body, "the holy Church throughout all the world', is broken into many fragments by the power of the Devil. (. . .) Some portions of it are altogether gone, and those that remain are separated from each other'.[31] The Anglican, the Greek and the Roman Church had, however, preserved objective unity while losing the subjective one. Within the Branch Theory each of these three Churches has a right to call itself Catholic; they are as truly Church as the

---

[27] H. E. Manning, *The Unity of the Church* (2nd edn, London, 1845), p. 162.

[28] Cf. ibid., p. 90

[29] Cf. ibid., p. 359

[30] J. H. Newman, 'On the Controversy with the Romanists', *Tracts for the Times*, n. 71 (1 Jan. 1836) (3rd edn, London, 1838), p. 29.

[31] J. H. Newman, *PPS*, iii, 14 (London, 1899), p. 191.

others, and they should recognise each other as sister Churches.[32] There was, however, a fact in need of explanation. Each one of these branches was a cluster of local churches brought together by political or geographical reasons, by reasons of expediency or co-operation, and so on: what is the ecclesiological nature of these groupings? Neither Newman nor Manning gave any indication as to the ecclesiological status of these branches of the Church. They seem to have felt that, from an ecclesiological point of view, these clusters of local churches added little or nothing to the theological concepts of local and universal Church.

Their last years in the Anglican Church were marked by a progressive distancing from the Branch Theory of Church unity. At the source of this change can be found their development of the idea of the Church as communion, with the law of love as the heart of the notion of communion. Manning, in particular, developed this concept at length on the basis of the pneumatological dimension of his ecclesiology. The love of God, he would say, has been poured into Christian souls by the Holy Spirit, and this divine love is the bond that holds together the mystical body of Christ, the cause of unity and the law of communion of the visible Church. This unity of love is a reflection in the Church of the unity of the three divine Persons, and Manning would add that Christ's visible body, physical as well as mystical, 'is the earthly clothing, the mystical impersonation of the love of God'.[33]

Manning perceived, against what he had previously held, that the communion of charity was an essential element of the Church's unity: 'It seems to me', he wrote to Gladstone in 1850, 'that indivisibleness of communion was held to be by a Divine necessity so that any person or portion falling off, or being in fact separate ceased to be of the Church; and yet the indivisible remainder was the Church as fully as before'.[34] He was even more explicit in a letter to Robert Wilberforce:

> The Faith of the Holy Trinity and of the Incarnation subdue me into a belief of the indivisible unity, and perpetual infallibility of the Body of Christ (. . .) I am forced to believe that the unity of His Person prescribes the unity of His visible kingdom as one, undivided whole; and that numbers are an accident. It was once contained in an upper chamber; it may be again; but it must always be one, and indivisible.[35]

[32] Cf. J. H. Newman, 'Catholicity of the Anglican Church', pp. 58–9; see also 'Controversy with the Romanists', p. 31.

[33] H. E. Manning, *ASer*, iv, p. 290.

[34] Manning to W. E. Gladstone, 5 September 1850, Manning MSS, Pitts Theology Library, Emory University, box 1, folder 9.

[35] Manning to R. Wilberforce, 28 December 1849, Manning MSS, Bodleian Library, Oxford, Eng. Lett. c. 655, fos 142 and 144.

There was another concept urging Newman and Manning towards a perception of Church unity beyond that provided by the Branch Theory. They came to give increasing relevance to St Cyprian's doctrine about the unity of the Episcopate in his *De Catholicae Ecclesiae Unitate* (Chapter 5): '*Episcopatus unus est, cuius a singulis in solidum pars tenetur*.' The Episcopate, in the translation of the Oxford Library of the Fathers, is 'one and undivided'; 'it is a whole in which each enjoys full possession'.[36] By 1844 Newman could write to his sister Jemima Mozley that:

> the 'Apostles are a council to *Christ* – but singly they are each a perfect type of Christ'. In like manner St. Cyprian's language is, that the episcopal power is shared by *all* bishops *fully*. His expression is '*in solidum*' which means like *joint tenure* or partnership, where each has full enjoyment of all prerogatives and the whole responsibility.[37]

This vision of the unity of the episcopate also facilitated a growing perception of the role played by the Roman Pontiff in the preservation of unity. The Branch Theory did acknowledge a certain primacy of honour for the Pope, as successor of Peter, while rejecting Rome's claims to universal jurisdiction or infallibility.[38] In 1843, however, Newman shocked Manning with his avowal that the Roman Church was the Catholic Church, and 'ours not a part of the Catholic Church, because not in communion with Rome'.[39] Two years later, in his *Development of Christian Doctrine* (1845), Newman claimed: 'We know of no other way of preserving the *Sacramentum Unitatis*, but a centre of unity.'[40] He had considered before how this need was met at local level by the bishop;[41] he now saw the Pope fulfilling the same role within the universal Church. Applying his theory of development, Newman affirmed that the powers and roles of Pope and bishops, although divinely bestowed, had been at first more or less dormant, and that, in the 'course of time, first the power of the bishop displayed itself, and then the power of the Pope'.[42] The process of that development had been determined by external circumstances and needs: 'local disturbances

---

[36] T. C. Cyprian, *Treatises*. Library of the Fathers of the Catholic Church anterior to the Division of the East and West, iii (Oxford, 1839), p. 134.

[37] Letter dated 19 April 1844, quoted in J. Tolhurst, *The Church*, p. 64.

[38] Cf. J. H. Newman, 'Catholicity of the Anglican Church', pp. 24–5; see also H. E. Manning, *Unity of the Church*, pp. 363–6.

[39] Newman to Manning, 25 October 1843, Manning MSS, Bodleian Library, c. 654, fos 52 and 53.

[40] J. H. Newman, *The Development of Christian Doctrine* (14th edn, London, 1909), pp. 154–5.

[41] Cf. J. H. Newman, MS Sermon 216, 15 November 1829, 'On Church Union and the Sin of Schism', pp. 2–3, quoted in J. Tolhurst, *The Church*, p. 48.

[42] J. H. Newman, *Development*, p. 149.

gave exercise to bishops, and next ecumenical disturbances gave exercise to Popes'.[43]

Manning, along the same lines, could ask in 1847: 'Is it not part of the revealed will and ordinance of our Lord Jesus Christ, that the Church should be under an episcopate united with a visible head, as the apostles were united with St Peter?' He clarified that he was not thinking, however, of the primacy of the Roman Pontiff, as understood by Roman theologians: 'It is not the question of primacy with me so much as *unity of the episcopate*. *"Episcopatus unus est."* I take St. Peter to have been the first of apostles, as the Primate of Christendom is the first of bishops; in spiritual order or power all being equal.'[44] On those bases, Manning would reject any concept of 'insularity' in respect of the Church, as when he wrote to Gladstone:

> Protestantism is heretical, and Nationalism is Judaic. I remember you saying that the English Monarchy is an idea wh[ich] commands the veneration and affections of your mind in a way beyond what I am likely to feel. On the other hand *'Tu es Petrus'*, and *'Credo in Unam C[a]th[olicam] Eccl[esia]m'* reveal to me a divine Monarchy claiming a sentiment of loyalty to a Person in Heaven before which all other kingdoms melt away.[45]

2. Ecclesiology from Vatican II to 'Dominus Jesus'

Manning's and Newman's ecclesiology paralleled more or less contemporary theological developments within the Catholic Church, particularly those in the theology of Johan Adam Möhler, whose insights into the theology of the mystical body of Christ present many points of contact with the ideas of Newman and Manning on the subject, and, like them, he had built his thought on a deep Patristic foundation.[46] This seam of a theology of the Church as the mystical body of Christ, which Möhler had started exploring, was later worked by other nineteenth-century Catholic theologians like the Jesuits Carlo Passaglia and Clement Shrader, their *De Ecclesia Christi* appeared in the years 1853–4. Shrader went on to play an

---

[43] Ibid., p. 151.

[44] Manning to C. Laprimaudaye, 16 June 1847, quoted in E. S. Purcell, *Life of Cardinal Manning, Archbishop of Westminster*, i (London, 1896), p. 471.

[45] Manning to Gladstone, 3 April 1848, Manning MSS, Pitts Library, box 1, folder 9.

[46] See G. Biemer, 'A Vivified Church: Common Structures in the Ecclesiology of Johan Adam Möhler and John Henry Newman,' *Internationale Cardinal-Newman-Studien*, xvi (Sonderdruck, 1998), pp. 240–68; also P. Erb's Introduction to his edition of J. A. Möhler, *Unity of the Church or The Principle of Catholicism. Presented in the Spirit of the Church Fathers of the First Three Centuries* (Washington: CUA Press, 1996), pp. 61–6; also J. Pereiro, *Cardinal Manning. An Intellectual Biography* (Oxford: Oxford University Press, 1998), pp. 43–4 and 118.

important part in the drafting of the first schema *De Ecclesia* presented to the Council Fathers in Vatican I, and to work very closely with Manning during the sessions of the Council. That first schema *De Ecclesia* was entirely based on the doctrine of the Mystical Body of Christ, and the opening chapter had precisely that title: *De Corpore Christi Mystici*. The criticisms of many of the Fathers, based mostly on juridical and sociological arguments, and the pressures imposed by the question of Papal infallibility, led to the abandonment of the schema. Partly because of this, a proper development of the theology of the mystical body of Christ, and its magisterial expression, would be delayed until well into the twentieth century. At a magisterial level, it fell to Pius XII, in his encyclical *Mystici Corporis Christi* (1943), and especially to Vatican II, to build on the preceding ecclesiological developments in the theology of the mystical body of Christ.

Vatican II, when referring to the formation of the Church, affirmed that, by 'communicating his Spirit, Christ mystically constitutes as his body those brothers of his who are called together from every nation. In that body the life of Christ is communicated to those who believe and who, through the sacraments, are united in a hidden and real way to Christ in his passion and glorification'.[47] The very notion of the Church as mystical body of Christ conveys the idea of communion, and this is so to such an extent that John Paul II could say that communion 'lies at the heart of the Church's self-understanding'.[48] Vatican II went on to say that this concept also lies at the heart of man's self-understanding, as a being created for communion, who finds her or his personal perfection in self-communication to others. Communion is the very *raison d'être* of the acts of creation and elevation: God calls men and women out of nothing to communion with him and with their fellows, a communion which finds its fulfilment in the Church: 'a people brought into unity from the unity of the Father, the Son and the Holy Spirit'.[49] By its very nature this concept of communion includes within itself the dimension of catholicity: it is offered to and open to all. Communion is catholic, or it simply does not exist.[50]

In the ecclesiology of Vatican II the concept of the Church as communion is closely related to that of the Church as *sacrament*. Besides being the organically structured community of those incorporated into the

[47] Vatican II, *Lumen Gentium*, 7.

[48] John Paul II, 'Address to the Bishops of the United States of America, 16 September 1987, no. 1: *Insegnamenti di Giovanni Paolo II*, X, 3 (1987), 553. Vatican II repeatedly used this term to describe the mystery of the Church (cf. *Lumen Gentium*, nn. 4, 8, 13–15, 18, 24–5; *Dei Verbum*, n. 10; *Unitatis Redintegratio*, nn. 2–4, 14–15, 17–19, 22).

[49] Vatican II, *Lumen Gentium*, 4.

[50] Cf. J. Ratzinger, *Called to Communion. Understanding the Church Today* (San Francisco: Ignatius Press, 1996), p. 82.

mystical body of Christ, the Church is endowed with the means to build up that union and add new members to itself. The Church grows, however, from within: she gives birth to new members in baptism, and the root and centre of the ecclesial communion is the Eucharist. Christ builds up the Church and keeps it alive through the Eucharist; this is 'the creative force and source of communion among the members of the Church, precisely because it unites each one of them with Christ himself (cf. 1 Cor. 10:17)'.[51] This centrality of the Holy Eucharist to the life of the Mystical Body of Christ establishes a clear connection between Christ's physical and mystical bodies: Christ gives us his body and, in so doing, makes us into one by engrafting us onto his body and making us live with his life. The physical body of Christ is the vine on which the branches are grafted, and they are kept alive and preserved in unity by the Eucharist. Thus, the ecclesiology of the mystical body of Christ has at its heart a eucharistic ecclesiology. The Eucharist makes the Church: it was born of the Cross, and it is maintained alive by the renewal of the sacrifice of Calvary. Not only is the Church born of the Eucharist, she is in herself a eucharistic community, and the Mass is her form; it defines the Church's fundamental constitution: 'the Church [is and] lives in eucharistic community'.[52]

This new emphasis on a eucharistic ecclesiology led, in its turn, to the paying of greater attention to the nature of the particular Church. Vatican II defined it as 'a section of the People of God entrusted to a bishop to be guided by him with the assistance of his clergy so that, loyal to its pastor and formed by him into one community in the Holy Spirit through the Gospel and the Eucharist, it constitutes one particular church in which the one, holy, catholic and apostolic Church of Christ is truly present and active'.[53] In the words of *Communionis notio*, particular Churches 'are in themselves *Churches*, because, although they are particular, the universal Church becomes present in them with all her essential elements'.[54] And that constitutive presence is the fruit of the Eucharist. In every celebration of the Eucharist the total Christ, physical and mystical, is really present; the Eucharist is a celebration of the whole Church by which it makes itself present within the particular community.

There is a mutual indwelling of the universal in the particular Church, and of the local in the universal Church. Particular Churches depend on the universal Church for the celebration of the Eucharist and for their very

---

[51] Congregation for the Doctrine of the Faith (CDF), *Communionis notio* (28 May 1992), (London: CTS, 1992), 5.

[52] J. Ratzinger, 'The Ecclesiology of Vatican II', *L'Osservatore Romano* (English edn), 25 November 1985, p. 8.

[53] Vatican II, *Christus Dominus*, 11.

[54] CDF, *Communionis Notio*, 7.

existence; they are, besides, 'constituted after the model of the universal Church'. On the other hand, 'it is in these [particular Churches] and formed out of them that the one and unique Catholic Church exists'.[55] The universal Church is a communion, a body of Churches. However – as mentioned in respect of individual Christians incorporated into the Church – the universal Church is not the product resulting from their coming together. In its 'essential mystery, it [the universal Church] is a reality *ontologically and temporally* prior to every *individual* particular Church'.[56] The universal Church was born in the Upper Room, on Pentecost day, and the twelve apostles, the representatives of the one unique Church, were the founders-to-be of the local churches.[57]

As a result, it is not possible to treat the universal Church and particular Churches as juxtaposed entities. In each particular Church there exists (*existit*) the universal Church, and it is in the particular Churches that the universal Church is present and active. In the words of a commentator, the 'mystery of the particular Church, in synthesis, is the mystery of the presence of the *whole* in the *part*, while the part still remains *part* of the *whole*'. The particular Church, therefore, 'cannot be conceived of as something "intermediary" between the faithful and the universal Church, in such a way that one would belong to the universal Church *through* the particular Church. On the contrary, belonging to a particular Church and belonging to the universal Church is one single two-dimensional Christian reality'. It has to be added, however, 'that one only participates in the universal Church by participating in the mystery of the particular Church, in which the universal Church *existit, inest, operatur*'.[58]

That mutual indwelling depends on the episcopal office at the centre of the local church, primarily as an essential component of the Eucharist. The Eucharist – consecrated by the bishop, or by priests in communion with him – makes present in that portion of the people of God which is the particular Church the Church universal. It is through Apostolic Succession that the power to make the universal Church present and active in the particular, constituting it into Church, is entrusted to the bishop. Eucharistic ecclesiology is thus intimately connected with the idea of episcopal collegiality, which also belongs, in the same measure, to the foundations of Vatican II's ecclesiology.[59] A bishop is not a bishop by himself, but only in Catholic communion with those who were bishops

[55] Vatican II, *Lumen Gentium*, 23.

[56] CDF, *Communionis Notio*, 9.

[57] Ibid.

[58] P. Rodríguez, *Particular Churches and Personal Prelatures* (Dublin: Four Courts Press, 1986), pp. 103 and 105–6; see also CDF, *Communionis Notio*, 10.

[59] Cf. J. Ratzinger, 'Ecclesiology of Vatican II', p. 9.

before him, with those who are bishops with him and with those who will be bishops after him. The bishops' offices of sanctifying, teaching and ruling 'of their very nature can be exercised only in hierarchical communion with the head and the members of the college'.[60] The unity of the Episcopate is no accident, but rather it expresses and realises the unity of the Church.[61]

Apostolic succession, therefore, is not the mere handing of certain powers to an individual, it involves his inclusion into a corporate order, the college of bishops. Collegiality belongs to the very essence of the episcopal ministry, as the bishops are not – except in the case of the bishop of Rome – successors of a particular apostle; they are rather the members of the college that takes the place of the apostolic college. As such, they have responsibility not only in respect to the particular Church in which they are centres of unity, but they also share *in solidum* in the '*sollicitudo omnium ecclesiarum*', in the anxious care for all the Churches. Each bishop is bound to have such concern and solicitude for the whole Church, and reflect it in every aspect of his pastoral ministry.[62] Within that concern for all the churches, the primary contribution of the bishops to the welfare of the universal Church is in fact through their service to their own Churches 'as portions of the universal Church, [in this way] they contribute efficaciously to the welfare of the whole Mystical Body, which, from another point of view, is a corporate body of Churches'.[63] The '*sollicitudo omnium ecclesiarum*', however, is not confined to the bishop. Through him the particular Church is to share in the concern for all the Churches, the natural result of its incorporation to the mystical body of Christ, in which all the different parts are to make each other's welfare their common care, and each individual part contributes through its special gifts to the good of the other parts and the whole Church.[64]

Vatican II would add that, 'in order that the episcopate itself, however, might be one and undivided he put Peter at the head of the other apostles, and in him he set up a lasting and visible source and foundation of the unity both of faith and of communion'.[65] The unity of communion of the visible Church requires a visible centre or focus; collegiality involves the existence of a bishop 'who is head of the body or college of bishops, namely the Roman Pontiff'.[66] A similar conclusion might be reached, perhaps, by starting from a consideration of the particular Churches, constituted after

[60] Vatican II, *Lumen Gentium*, 21.
[61] Cf. ibid., nn. 18, 21, 22.
[62] Cf. ibid., 23.
[63] Ibid.
[64] Cf. ibid., 13; cf. 1 Corinthians 12:26.
[65] Vatican II, *Lumen Gentium*, 18.
[66] CDF, *Communionis Notio*, 12.

the model of the universal Church. The bishop is the visible source and foundation of unity in the particular Church; in the universal Church there is a corresponding perpetual and visible source and foundation of unity, namely the successor of Peter.[67] In Newman's words: 'What a bishop is to his Church – such the Pope to all the bishops and the whole Church. A Bishop of Bishops.'[68] The mission of the bishop of Rome within the college consists precisely in 'keeping watch' (*episkopein*) over whatever relates to the unity of the Church: the handing down of the word, the celebration of the liturgy and sacraments, the mission of the Church, etc. 'With the power and the authority without which such an office would be illusory, the bishop of Rome must ensure the communion of all the Churches.'[69] This is a service of love which, while preserving what is essential to its mission, is always open to new situations and may express itself in various ways.[70] The unity of the Eucharist and the unity of the Episcopate *with Peter and under Peter* cannot be considered as independent roots of the unity of the Church, since Christ instituted the Eucharist and the episcopate as essentially interlinked realities.

The presence of the universal Church in the particular one implies that the Pope, and his service to unity, are not external to the local church, but an integral part of it. For a particular Church 'to be fully Church, that is, the particular presence of the universal Church with all its essential elements, and hence constituted *after the model of the universal Church*, there must be present in it, as a proper element, the supreme authority of the Church: the episcopal college "together with their head, the Supreme Pontiff, and never apart from him"';[71] communion with Rome is an essential requisite of full and visible communion. Radically, every valid celebration of the Eucharist expresses communion with the whole Church, and therefore with Peter, or objectively, by its own very nature, it calls for it.[72] Again, this presence and service of the universal Church in the particular may take different forms in response to diverse times and circumstances.

The Church, therefore, is not a goal which all particular Churches must strive to reach. The Universal Church pre-existed particular ones: these are born of her, and she survives their disappearance or separation. As such, the Catholic Church cannot be divided. Individuals and groups may separate themselves from her in different ways and degrees, but she always

---

[67] Cf. Vatican II, *Lumen Gentium*, 23.

[68] J. H. Newman, Theo. Paper VIII, 25 February 1866, in *Theological Papers on Inspiration and Infallibility*, J. D. Holmes (ed.) (Oxford: Oxford University Press, 1979), p. 110.

[69] John Paul II, *Ut Unum Sint* (25 May 1995) (London: CTS, 1995), n. 94.

[70] Cf. ibid., n. 95

[71] CDF, *Communionis Notio*, 13.

[72] Ibid., 14.

remains one and whole, irrespective of the number of particular Churches in communion with her: 'the Church of Christ, despite the divisions which exist among Christians, continues to exist fully only in the Catholic Church'.[73] *Dominus Jesus*, quoting Vatican II, added that this is the single Church entrusted to Peter and the Apostles, and that there is an historical continuity – rooted in the apostolic succession – between the Church founded by Christ and the Catholic Church: 'this Church constituted and organised as a society in the present world, subsists in [*subsistit in*] the Catholic Church, governed by the Successor of Peter and by the bishops in communion with him'.[74]

The determination of the proper meaning of the word *subsists*, as used by *Lumen Gentium*, has given rise to a considerable amount of discussion. The term was chosen, on the one hand, to clarify that there exists only one 'subsistence' of the true Church, a single Church of Christ. A second reason for the use of this expression was to avoid possible terminological imprecision originating in words used by Pius XII, in his Encyclical *Mystici Corporis Christi* (1943). There he said that the true Church of Christ *is* the Holy, Catholic Apostolic, Roman Church. It was feared that that *is* could be perceived as expressing complete identity between the Catholic Church and the universal Church, as if there was no Church outside the Catholic one. This interpretation would not properly express the Catholic teaching that local churches separated from Rome are true local churches. *Dominus Jesus* acknowledged this fact: 'the Church of Christ is present and operative also in these Churches, even though they lack full communion with the Catholic Church'.[75] The Council added an important qualification to the effect that it is precisely because the Catholic Church is present in them, through apostolic succession and the Eucharist, that they are constituted in Churches and possess the virtualities of the universal Church.

John Paul II, following in the footsteps of Vatican II and early tradition, has made repeated use of the expression 'sister churches' to refer to particular or local churches.[76] The expression involves a theological category. It is not a mere form of affectionate or stereotyped courteous form of address, and its richness and ecumenical value demand respect for its full and proper meaning. Newman, within the context of the Branch Theory, had spoken of sister Churches, establishing a relationship of equality between the Anglican, Orthodox and Roman Churches. This can hardly find a place in

---

[73] CDF, Declaration *Dominus Jesus* (6 Aug. 2000) (London: CTS, 2000), 16.

[74] Ibid., 16; quoting Vatican II, *Lumen Gentium*, 8.

[75] CDF, *Dominus Jesus*, 17.

[76] Cf. John Paul II, *Ut Unum Sint*, nn. 56 and 60; *Slavorum Apostoli* (2 June 1985), 27 (London: CTS, 1985).

the ecclesiology of Vatican II. According to its principles, the universal Catholic Church is not something of the past or else of a future to be hoped for; it is here and now, visible, in a substantial continuity – or 'personal identity' – with the Church founded by Christ. It may increase in respect of the number of its parts, and some may separate or remain only loosely attached to it, but this does not detract from its substantial completeness. In the words of the Congregation for the Doctrine of the Faith's note on 'Sister Churches': the 'Catholic and apostolic Universal Church is not sister but *mother* of all the particular Churches'.[77] A proper and true sisterhood of equality can only be established among particular Churches or groups of Churches (patriarchates or metropolitan provinces). It is not without significance – a significance worthy of further study – that the Pope is the head of the universal Church by virtue of being, as successor of St Peter, the bishop of a particular Church, the Church in Rome, sister of all other particular Churches.[78]

Those ecclesial communities which, for whatever reason, have not preserved the valid Episcopate – and lack, therefore, the genuine and integral substance of the Eucharistic mystery – are not particular Churches in the proper sense of the word, although the term Church is sometimes used when referring to them.[79] Their ecclesiological status is, at present, difficult to define and in need of detailed study. However, speaking of them, and of particular Churches not in communion with Rome, Vatican II clearly said that 'the Spirit of Christ has not refrained from using them as means of salvation which derived their efficacy from the very fullness of grace and truth entrusted to the Catholic Church'.[80] They may make positive contributions, in particular cases, to the life or understanding of the Catholic Church, and may even be used by God to further important aspects of his providential designs for the universal Church. However, as Ratzinger has pointed out, 'the fact that God can make division yield positive fruits does not make it positive in itself'.[81] It goes without saying that, even if those communities cannot be termed 'sister Churches', their members cannot be other than sisters and brothers in the faith in Jesus Christ.

At this point, the image of the mystical body of Christ, so useful to describe the mystery of communion within the Church, was found incapable of expressing properly the different degrees of membership of the Church:

[77] CDF, Note 'Sister Churches' (30 June 2000), published in *The Tablet* (9 Sept. 2000), p. 1206.

[78] Cf. ibid.

[79] Cf. CDF, *Dominus Jesus*, 17.

[80] Vatican II, *Unitatis Redintegratio*, 3.

[81] Interview published in *Frankfurter Allgemeine Zeitung* (20 Sept. 2000), English translation in *L'Osservatore Romano*, 6 December 2000, p. 8.

membership of a body does not admit degrees – one is a member or one is not – and, consequently, non-Catholics would be completely excluded from communion with the Church. Vatican II clearly affirmed that the Church knows that she is joined in many ways to those who are baptised but do not profess the Catholic faith or have not preserved communion under the successor of Peter, and the Council found the concept 'People of God' more flexible in this respect than that of the mystical body of Christ.[82] Manning and Newman might perhaps have used in this respect another gospel image, that of the union of the branches and the vine, where there can be dried up branches or others which, more or less united to the trunk and depending on the amount of sap flowing into them, do still bud and produce fruits of sanctity.

*   *   *

Perhaps the first thing to point out in these final remarks is the significant convergence of Tractarian and Catholic theologies on the ecclesiological notion of the mystical body of Christ, eucharistic ecclesiology, and so on. There are also obvious areas which Newman and Manning did not fully explore, particularly when it came to relations between the particular and the universal Church, the bishop's role in this respect, and the Petrine office. Even here it is possible to find hints and distant views of a way forward. The shared foundation of these ecclesiologies (the Newman–Manning Anglican and the Catholic) could perhaps offer a basis for further ecumenical dialogue. Within this study, it would be useful to engage in further research concerning the extent to which the Tractarian theology of the mystical body found continuity and achieved further development within Anglican theology, and to determine whether and how those almost contemporary and parallel lines of development started to separate from each other, and what were the reasons for that divergence.

---

[82] Cf. Vatican II, *Lumen Gentium*, 15 and 16. There were other ecclesiological truths – like the radical equality and common priesthood of the faithful – which also found more adequate expression within the concept of People of God.

Book Reviews

Gunnel Borgegård, Olav Fanuelsen, Christine Hall (ed.), *The Ministry of the Deacon, 2. Ecclesiological Explorations* (Uppsala: Nordic Ecumenical Council, 2000), 91–85564–10–9, 285 pp.

The Ministry of the Deacon: Ecclesiological Explorations is the second of three projected volumes within the Anglo-Nordic Diaconal Research Project (ANDREP). Since ANDREP had undertaken this project only in January 1997, publication of volume two before the end of 2000 is something of a phenomenon in itself and says much for the vigour with which questions about the modern diaconate are being pursued at this time.

The first volume had appeared a little over twelve months previously under the same editors (less Olav Fanuelsen) but was of less general interest than the present volume. As its subtitle *Anglican-Lutheran Perspectives* indicated, the first volume was aiming to provide information about the diaconate within the participating Church bodies of ANDREP, the Church of England, the Church of Norway, the Church of Sweden, and the Evangelical-Lutheran Church of Finland. One helpful extra, however, was backgrounding about ANDREP by Christine Hall, co-editor, Director of the Bishop Otter Centre for Theology and Ministry in Chichester, and one of the modern champions of the diaconate. Another – of lasting value – was the historical survey by Sven-Erik Brodd, Dean of the Faculty of Theology in the University of Uppsala, of the 'phenomenon' of the diaconate's rise and rise (his other contribution was a lengthy report and searching critique of the Swedish diaconate). In addition, bibliographies arranged by language of publication facilitate access to books and Church reports that are sometimes awkward to track down.

This was all in the line of a statement of position. Even so, within this refreshing ecumenical initiative, one could observe denominational varieties of diaconate (or of deacon, to use a less 'Catholic' term) and indeed not a few seeming incompatibilities. But this was one objective of the project: to get all the bits and pieces on the table. Hence the second volume, and, after this, a third, which is already in preparation to complete this 'diaconal research project'.

A first reservation could easily suggest itself. With such a strong Lutheran presence through three Nordic Churches, why do we not see participation from the Evangelical Church of Germany (Lutheran), which mothered the modern diaconate? This Church continues to host a vast diaconal operation which, from the middle of the nineteenth century, seeded similar operations in Lutheran Churches of central and northern Europe. The question suggests itself also because the only non-Lutheran participating Church in ANDREP, the Church of England, had already engaged with the Lutheran World Federation, via the Anglican-Lutheran International Commission, in the production of the Hanover Report *The Diaconate as Ecumenical Opportunity* (1996), a document notable for significant new departures in thinking about the diaconate.

Indications already exist in ANDREP's first volume, however, as to why the Nordic-Anglican arrangement was better so. These pointed to increasing pressures in ecumenical quarters to find an 'ecclesial' place for deacons in the Church. Tautologous as this might sound, a genuinely ecclesial recognition of deacons would lead, as Professor Brodd put it, to opening up within Protestant traditions 'the possibility of more than one ordained ministry'. In regard to deacons this happened within the Church of Sweden in 1999, although there they prefer to think of it as a diaconate functioning within the one ordained ministry, and also, but less remarkably, within the Church of England in 1987 with the introduction of the distinctive diaconate alongside the traditional transitional diaconate. Within German Lutheranism, by contrast, from the very beginnings such an ecclesial incorporation of deacons has never been a realistic objective. The authenticity of the German Lutheran deacon derives not from an ordination but from the authenticity of the *diakonia* itself which the deacon exhibits in loving service, albeit under the blessing of the Church. Only in 2001 has the German diaconal movement begun an exploratory review. With roots in its nineteenth-century foundations still strong, the German diaconal organisations would not have known where to turn once ANDREP indicated the direction in which it was likely to move. Tensions engendered by a drift towards ordination of deacons are acknowledged in the Hanover Report itself.

The Hanover Report none the less drew sharp attention to a shift of orientation in its thinking about deacons. It spoke of deacons less as loving servants of those in need than as 'agents ordained to assist . . . in the proclamation and celebration of Word and Sacrament . . .', and it attributed this new orientation to 'the historical-philological corrective to earlier understandings' of *diakonia* and other 'deacon' words which my research volume of 1990 had provided, *Diakonia: Reinterpreting the Ancient Sources*. In the first ANDREP volume both Brodd and Hall pointed to the same research as raising questions about 'concentration on the charitable task of the deacon' to the loss of the deacon's ecclesial connection. A working party within the Church of England itself has since completed a review of the diaconate (due for release September 2001) which took its rise from similar misgivings.

With such new perspectives already taking shape, ANDREP's second volume moves into its main work with further probings by Sven-Erik Brodd in a paper which examines interconnections between concepts of *caritas* and *diakonia*. The former Latin term comprises, of course, the charitable works which the nineteenth-century founders of the diaconal movement presented as the defining role of deacons but which they then confusingly named *diakonia*. A habit of language quickly developed out of this misnomer, and it has shown itself to be not easily eradicable. In confronting the issue by distinguishing *caritas* from *diakonia*, Brodd is able to locate *diakonia* not in acts of love but in activity resulting from the ecclesial bonding established between deacon and Church by ordination.

Robert Hannaford expands at length on Brodd's call for a revamped *diakonia* by rehearsing the philological story of the term and warning of theological impasses if we continue to think of ministry as part of 'the undifferentiated responsibility of all Christian individuals'. Taking a lead from the new lexical description of *diakonia* – which has since received the independent endorsement of Frederick Danker's third English-language edition of Walter Bauer's *Greek-English Lexicon of the New Testament and Other Early Christian Literature* (2000) – Hannaford explores critical implications of the new lexical description for the ecclesial identity of the deacon. He establishes that identity in the deacon's ministry 'summons to some particular, explicit, work for and on behalf of the Church' (p. 250), where the summons establishes a role which is both representational of the Church and relational in regard to the rest of the ordained ministry.

In this Hannaford has put the fullest and strongest case to date for full recognition of the deacon in both Church and theology. From a pastoral perspective, Kjell Nordstokke challenges the Church to review its own identity by reflecting on the prophetic diaconal activity occurring on its peripheries and thereby to develop a sense of its corporate responsibility for the social transformation of societies. Will such a call resonate through synod deliberations?

All these are mainly innovative attitudes with which to address issues of the diaconate today, and in this volume they are knowingly, even vigorously, projected in the face of deeply entrenched traditional views which are by no means wholly compatible with them. Thus the book looks beyond the methodologies and theological approaches represented in even the wide scholarship of Dorothea Reininger's *Diakonat der Frau* (1999).

The perspectives selected for closer attention in this review are not the only important perspectives in this collection of papers – where we also encounter a broad overview of ecclesiology (Risto Ahonen), a comparative study of vocational training (Olav Fanuelsen), and a timely insistence on 'the significance of the liturgical-social axis of the deacon's ministry' (Christine Hall) – but deacons would want to see a prompt clarification of the issues raised here because their resolution intimately affects the deacons' sense of identity. Indeed, Ninni Smedberg points out that a sense of identity has long been elusive for deacons. So often they are cast adrift in the Church or in the arena of their social engagement with nothing more to support their spirituality than what they brought with them from their pre-deacon days.

Many have been the second thoughts on the part of ecclesiastical authorities in regard to the introduction of deacons to today's churches. Signs of such uncertainties have been the wildly uneven spread of new deacons within those churches which have left the introduction of deacons to the discretion of local authorities. Further telltale signs have been ambivalent attitudes in regard to deacons' place in the order of the Church and, related to that, the unequal adaptations of the nineteenth-century diaconate to the new social conditions applying over the last forty years. Interestingly, it is from within the latter environment that the initiatives taken by ANDREP have largely developed. These initiatives are potentially groundbreaking and, as constituted of theological reflections and explorations, stand in strong contrast to the largely canonical and administrative measures developed by the Vatican's major review of the diaconate and enshrined in *The Permanent Diaconate. Basic Norms for the Formation of Permanent Deacons* and *Directory for the Ministry and Life of Permanent Deacons* (1998). Much of ANDREP's initiative has arisen on the basis of the vision expressed in the Porvoo declaration of 1992 and in the commitment of the Porvoo Churches represented in ANDREP 'to work towards a common understanding of diaconal ministry'. Their objective is not yet fully achieved, and we look forward to where their reflections in this second volume lead them in their third.

JOHN N. COLLINS

Dennis M. Doyle, *Communion Ecclesiology* (Maryknoll, New York: Orbis Books, 2000) 1–57075–327–X, ix + 195 pp.

Communion ecclesiology has gained in importance amongst theologians of all the main Christian traditions. Not only that, it has also become a significant factor in official Church documents and in various ecumenical statements. In the Roman Catholic Church the Extraordinary Synod of 1985, which met to survey progress in implementing Vatican II described communion ecclesiology as the key to a proper understanding of the Council documents. J. M. R. Tillard who described *koinonia* as 'the horizontal line around which the major ecclesiological affirmations of the Second Vatican Council revolve' echoes this view [*Church of Churches: The Ecclesiology of Communion*, p. xi]. On the ecumenical front the World Council of Churches statement *The Unity of the Church as Koinonia: Gift and Calling*, issued following the Canberra assembly in 1991, identified *koinonia* as basic to the Church's mission and identity. The understanding of the Church as Communion is also the key idea in most of the bilateral dialogues between different Churches. The Anglican Roman Catholic International Commission is a case in point. In its 1991 agreed statement *Church as Communion* the Commission responded to requests for clarification on the ecclesiological basis of its work, presenting a comprehensive reflection on *koinonia* as the central mystery of the Church's identity.

This growing consensus reflects a deeper perception that communion is fundamental to the being and identity of the Church. Pope John Paul the Second's statement that 'Communion is the very mystery of the Church' in *Christifideles laici* is an example of this. Communion is the form and basis of the eschatological community of salvation. Ecclesial communion is an anticipation of God's plan to bring all things into communion with him. It is not merely a hope for the future but the central defining feature of the Church's life. This approach to ecclesiology has not gone unchallenged. For Nicholas M. Healey it represents an idealised view of the Church, divorced from the actual historic experience of Christian people. This is an over-simplistic reaction. The Church has both an historical and an eschatological existence. Although the Church's history includes division and conflict, this is not the end of the matter. As the community of the Spirit, the Church also exists from the *eschaton*. Its story is also the story of Christ and the Spirit. This is not an idealisation against history. The Church's story is a participation in the divine engagement with history. As with the history of Jesus the story of the Church unfolds from the resurrection. The ecclesiology of communion offers a way of exploring the eschatological dialectic between promise and fulfilment in the life of the Church. The Church is not identical with the kingdom but it proclaims the promise of the kingdom and, in its *koinonia*, already anticipates its fulfilment. It is simultaneously a sign and instrument of the hoped-for kingdom and a foretaste and anticipation of the fulfilment of the kingdom. Set within history it none the less has its existence from that which is beyond history.

Denis Doyle's book is a welcome addition to the literature in this area of contemporary ecclesiology. Although communion is the basic form of the Church Doyle insists that this conceptualisation can accommodate a range of interpretations. Writing from a Catholic perspective he explores the diversity within his own tradition, noting that communion ecclesiology is embraced by radicals and conservatives alike. This goes some way towards refuting those who see communion ecclesiology as restrictive and essentialist. Doyle takes the communion ecclesiology of Vatican II as normative and shows how it has provided support both for those who stress *ressourcement* (the return to sources) and *aggiornamento* (updating). This insight establishes his basic methodology, which is to create a dialogue amongst (mostly) Catholic writers on the topic. The book identifies six different versions of communion ecclesiology: a Congregation for the Doctrine of the Faith version, a Rahnerian version, a Balthasarian version; a liberation version, a contextual version, and a reforming version. This diversity is seen an illustration of the comprehensive nature of communion ecclesiology. As Doyle argues communion ecclesiology has its roots in an earlier Catholic Mystical Body ecclesiology but since the Council it has broadened to embrace the sacramental and historical dimensions of the Church as well. Communion is not simply a feature of the juridical and institutional nature of the Church. It also includes the many different relationships that constitute the historical life of the Church. Communion ecclesiology takes us beyond the rather sterile division between the visible and the invisible since it stresses that the Church is both the receiver of revelation and also a vehicle for the revelation of God itself.

This is an extremely useful book. It provides the reader with a clear and accessible account of an important strain in modern Catholic theology. Doyle provides a detailed and systematic analysis of the main Catholic writers on this theme. Reference is also made to non-Catholic thinkers. For example, early in the book Doyle identifies the Protestant theologian Friedrich Schleiermacher as a seminal figure in the development of communion ecclesiology alongside the Catholic theologian Johann Adam Mohler. Doyle establishes that ecclesiology was fundamental for the theological method of both theologians. Both saw the Church and its unity as an intrinsic dimension of revelation and not merely a consequence of it. In discussing the patristic roots of communion ecclesiology Doyle also brings the orthodox theologian John Zizioulas and the Free Church theologian Miroslav Volf into the discussion. While drawing different conclusions about the nature of the Church both theologians ground their ecclesiology in the theology of the trinity. Doyle's vision of an inclusive communion ecclesiology is attractive. The reader will need to decide whether or not it is able the bear the weight of the task that Doyle envisages for it. A multidimensional communion ecclesiology might be taken by some as a contradiction in terms.

ROBERT HANNAFORD
University College Chichester

Nicholas M. Healy, *Church, World and the Christian Life: Practical-Prophetic Ecclesiology*. Cambridge Studies in Christian Doctrine 7 (Cambridge: Cambridge University Press, 2000), 0–521–78650–9 (pbk), 199 pp.

Like Alfred Loisy at the beginning of the twentieth century, Nicholas Healy sees the Church as continuously changing in response to changes in the social and cultural contexts in which it is set. Like Adolf Harnack, he believes the essence of Christianity to lie in the New Testament, and he argues that the task of ecclesiology should be to serve the Church's mission. That mission is to witness to the ultimate truth of salvation through Christ, and to foster discipleship committed to living out this truth. The ecclesiology he advocates is *practical* in that it addresses the Church's concrete existence with all its confusions, complexities and sinfulness. It is *prophetic* in bringing to bear critical and constructive judgements on the basis of 'Paul's rule', that is, of glorying only in Christ crucified (Gal. 6:14).

As would be expected at the start of the twenty-first century, Healy moves beyond the debates of modernism, and accepts the post-modern ('Neo-Nietzschean') view that there can be no 'impartial observer'. Instead, he argues that it is possible to establish truth from within a tradition. One of the tasks of ecclesiology is accordingly to make explicit the overarching worldview, metanarrative, or 'horizon' by which its practitioners seek to make sense of reality. Healy's preference is for a 'theodramatic horizon', an idea he adapts from Balthasar. This allows for 'genuine dialogue' within the drama of the mutual interaction between God, the Church and the world by those whose perspective is that of participants.

An ecclesiology which focuses on the Church's participation in the ongoing theodrama stands in sharp contrast to 'blueprint' ecclesiologies, like those which see the Church as 'sacrament' (Rahner), 'Body of Christ' (Barth), or 'communion' (Tillard). Such 'epic' approaches can never succeed in encapsulating the Church within a single model, because they can neither do justice to the variety of images in the New Testament, nor, individually, achieve a fully trinitarian perspective. Further, by their focus on the abstract, the ideal and the normative such ecclesiologies detract attention from the Church's actual historical existence in favour of its eschatological perfection.

Healy seeks to combine the biblically based conviction that Jesus Christ is the ultimate truth with an epistemology that maintains, on the one hand, that truth is not established by correspondence with some external abstract norm (pluralism thus fails), and, which, on the other hand, rejects the post-modern claim that all truth is relative, a stance which he considers 'irresponsible'. (Though deconstructionists might be allowed a playful smile at the frequency with which he describes the ever-changing Church as 'concrete'). Rather, following Alistair MacIntyre, he argues that the truth of a traditioned position, such as that of the Christian Church, must be established on the basis of its internal coherence and of successful explanatory power in its defence against challenges from those who differ. For Healy, truth is not the *possession* of the Church embodied in a set of doctrines, but is *received* from Christ, refracted through the action of the Holy Spirit in the Church-world 'concursus'. He thus argues that it is possible for the Church to be uncompromising in maintaining the superiority of its distinctive orientation towards Christ, the ultimate truth, while at the same time being respectful of genuine differences on the part of others, among whom the Spirit is also at work.

There is, however, a certain imbalance in the space devoted to ways of construing relations with other religions at the expense of consideration of the Church's interaction with its own heritage, and with those who challenge its views from within. Indeed, Healy's relentless deconstruction of alternative approaches in defence of his own, and his spirited affirmation of the superiority of Christianity over other religions, makes it difficult to see how the Holy Spirit can be recognised at work among them. Nor is it clear to what extent the new method of ecclesiology proposed is dependent upon his view of the Church, or upon the narrow New Testament basis which imparts such evangelistic zeal to his approach. The notion that the Church is continually reconstructing itself and the claim that it is inherently sinful are likely to raise as many hackles in traditional quarters today as did Loisy in his – or even to make Newman turn in his grave! Nevertheless, Healy sets out a challenging proposal to get ecclesiology off the drawing board and into the streets. It would be interesting to see it tested out in practice.

ALLAN K. JENKINS
University College, Chichester

Books Received

This listing includes some of the books which will be reviewed in forthcoming issues of the *International Journal for the Study of the Christian Church* and a selection of books received which, though space may not permit us to review them, are likely to be of interest to readers of this journal.

AVIS, PAUL, *The Anglican Understanding of the Church: an Introduction* (SPCK, 2000). ISBN 0 281 05282 4.

AVIS, PAUL, *Church, State and Establishment* (SPCK, 2001). ISBN 0 281 05404 5.

BLÜCKERT, KJELL, *The Church as Nation* (European University Studies, Peter Lang, Frankfurt am Main, 2000). ISBN 3 631 36168 8.

BROWN, STEWART and NEWLANDS, GEORGE (eds), *Scottish Christianity in the Modern World* (T&T Clark, 2001). ISBN 0 567 08765 4.

COLLINS, P. M., *Trinitarian Theology West and East: Karl Barth, the Cappadocian Fathers and John Zizioulas* (OUP, 2001). ISBN 0 19 827032 1.

FITZGERALD, KYRIAKI K., *Women Deacons in the Orthodox Church: Called to Holiness and Ministry* (Holy Cross Orthodox Press, 1998). ISBN 1 885652 22 4.

For Such a Time as this: a Renewed Diaconate in the Church of England (Church House Publishing, 2001). ISBN 0 715157 64 7.

GUNTON, COLIN E., *Theology through Preaching* (T&T Clark, 2001). ISBN 0 567 08774 3.

GUNTON, COLIN E. and HARDY, DANIEL W., *On Being the Church: Essays on the Christian Community* (T&T Clark, 2000). ISBN 0 567 29501 X.

HARDY, DANIEL W., *Finding the Church: the Dynamic Truth of Anglicanism* (SCM Press, 2001). ISBN 0 334 02863 9.

IRVIN, DALE T., and SUNQUIST SCOTT, W., *History of the World Christian Movement* (T&T Clark, 2001). ISBN 0 567 08866 9.

LEGRANDE, HERVÉ and THÉOBALD, CHRISTOPHE, *Le Ministère des Evêques au Concile Vatican II et depuis* (Editions du Cerf, Paris, France, 2001). ISBN 2 204 06723 7.

MÜLLER, GERHARD LUDWIG, *Priestertum und Diakonat* (Johannes Verlag Einsiedeln, Freiburg, 2000). ISBN 3 89411 360 X.

ROWELL, GEOFFREY, STEVENSON, KENNETH and WILLIAMS, ROWAN, *Love's Redeeming Work: the Anglican Quest for Holiness* (OUP, 2001). ISBN 0 19 122476 6.

SCERRI, HECTOR, *Koinonia, Diakonia and Martyria: Interrelated Themes in Patristic Sacramental Theology, as expounded by Adalbert G. Hamman*, OFM (Melita Theologica Supplementary Series 4, Malta, 1999). ISBN 99932 0 008 5.

Synode des Evêques, Rome, octobre, 2001, *L'Evêque, Serviteur de l'Evangile de Jésus Christ pour l'Espérance du Monde: Instrumentum Laboris*, 10ième Assemblée Générale Ordinaire, Rome, octobre, 2001 – Présentation par Mgr Jean-Pierre Ricard (Editions du Cerf, 2001). ISBN 2 204 06832 2.